uidebooks to the Museu d'Arqueologia de Catalunya

# EMPÚRIES

Xavier Aquilué
Pere Castanyer
Marta Santos
Joaquim Tremoleda

**Empúries**
Museu d'Arqueologia
de Catalunya

Generalitat
de Catalunya

Edicions
EL MÈDOL

# Índex

6    **The Emporitan topography.**

11   **Pre-colonial Empúries.**

15   **The arrival of the Phocaeans: the *Palaiapolis*.**

20   **The city on terra firma: the Neapolis.**

28   The city defences.

31   The area of the sanctuaries : the worship of Asclepius.

36   The Greek necropolises.

39   Economy and commerce.

44   ***Emporion* in the context of the Punic Wars and the arrival of the Romans.**

48   The city walls and the reforms in the religious area.

51   Agora and stoa.

54   Domestic architecture in the Neapolis.

56   The Hellenistic breakwater.

58   **The last modifications to the public areas of the Neapolis and other buildings of interest.**

64   The public cistern.

65   The salting factory.

66   The excavations in the car park.

## Index of the places of interest shown on the plans of the Guidebook

**NEAPOLIS**

1. Excavations in the car park, pp. 66-67
2. Walls and the entrance gate to the Neapolis, pp. 48-49
3. Area dedicated to Asclepius, (see the plan on page 29)
    3a) The 5th – 4th century BC extra-urban sanctuary, pp. 31-32
    3b) The temple to Asclepius, p. 33
    3c) Altar X, p. 33
    3d) Altar with a double altar-stone, 2nd –1st century BC, p. 33
    3e) The *Abaton* or lower terrace, pp. 49-50
    3f) The temple P, pp. 59-60
    3g) The cistern with four compartments, pp. 60-61
4. The temple to Isis and Zeus Serapis, pp. 61-63
5. 3rd century *proteichisma* or defensive reinforcement, pp. 44-45
6. 4th century BC wall and tower, pp. 28-31
7. The Torre Talaia, p. 25
8. House with the tetrastyle atrium, pp. 55-56
9. Tuscan atrium house, pp. 55-56
10. The salting factory, pp. 65-66
11. Peristyle house, p. 55
12. Public cistern and *macellum*, p. 64
13. Agora, pp. 51-53
14. Stoa, pp. 53-54
15. Paleo-Christian basilica, pp. 104-106
16. House with the Greek inscription ΗΔΥΚΟΙΤΟΣ, p. 56
17. House of the inscriptions, p. 56
18. Port, pp. 56-57
19. The port jetty, pp. 57-58
20. *Palaiapolis*, pp. 16-18

**ROMAN CITY**

21. Roman house no. 1
    -Late Republican period, pp. 82-84
    -Later extensions, pp. 93-96
22. Roman house no. 2A, p. 85
23. Roman house no. 2B
    -Late Republican atrium sector, p. 85
    -Later reforms to the house, p. 96
24. *Cardo* B, pp. 75-76
25. Forum
-Late Republican period (see plan on page 76)
    25a) Capitoline temple pp. 78-80
    25b) *Tabernae*, p. 78
    25c) Cryptoportico and portico, pp. 80-81
-Augustan Reform (see plan on page 91)
    25d) Capitoline temple, p. 89
    25e) Ambulacrum and area, p. 90
    25f) Basilica, pp. 90-91
    25g) Curia, p. 91
    25k) *Tabernae* in the south and the west sector, p. 90
    25l) Reform to the religious area, p. 92
26. *Cardo Maximus*, p. 77
27. *Insula* to the southeast of the forum, pp. 97-98
28. Main entrance gate and south wall, pp. 73-74
29. Amphitheatre, pp. 99-100
30. Palaestra, p. 100
*31. Church of Santa Margarida, pp. 109-111
*32. Church of Santa Magdalena, p. 109
*33. Les Corts hill, p. 70
*34. Church of Sant Vicenç, pp. 111-112

* Areas 31,32,33 and 34 can be found on the plan on page 9.

The numbers shown on the plan correspond to the points of interest along the route. The page numbers have been added so that you can follow the explanation in this guidebook.

**A** Museum
**B** Audiovisual room
**C** Shop
**D** Educational resources room

Entrance
**P** Car Park
Service road
Access
Pedestrian path
Bar
**C** Public telephone
Lavatories

18

## Ancient port

19

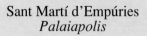

## Sant Martí d'Empúries
*Palaiapolis*

20

## The Emporitan topography

Throughout the history of Empúries, various settlements were established which were not always active simultaneously. This multiplicity is the element that makes this site a unique place for researching and discovering classical culture in Catalonia. Therefore, it is useful for visitors to have a little knowledge about the topography and the situation of the various settlements that today make up the archaeological site of Empúries, some of which are outside the itinerary of this site.

The changes in the landscape have led to considerable changes in the appearance of the Empordà region and therefore in that of the Emporitan area of the past. Ancient topography shows this coastal sector to the

Aerial view of the marshes that can still be seen today in the Alt Empordà region, allowing us to imagine the appearance these lands must have had in the 6<sup>th</sup> century BC.

south of the Bay of Roses as an area of low land full of swamps and marshes, which were flooded most of the year, and which became filled in over time due to the constant build up of river sediment from the Rivers Muga, Fluvià and Ter. Several hills overlooked this unusable territory, including those which would later serve as nuclei for the settlements in Empúries.

Geologically speaking, these were the last northern outcrops of the calcareous massif of Montgrí, and they were mainly made up of a great platform on which the Greek and Roman cities were founded. To the south the boundary of this hill was the former course of the River Ter, and to the west "Les Corts" hill, to which it was joined by means of a narrow pass. To the north, there was a different rocky outcrop that was smaller and in the past had been linked to the mainland by an isthmus, which gave it the appearance of a real island, and which was chosen by the Greeks to establish their first settlement (the *Palaiapolis*, the present day village of Sant Martí d'Empúries). Between these two high points there was a small natural bay that was the main port for the city. Further to the north there was the previous mouth of the River Fluvià.

The topographical reconstruction of these elements is essential to be able to understand the development of the Emporitan settlements, as it has not been easy to put aside a series of beliefs deeply rooted in a tradition that goes back to the Middle Ages. One of the most significant was the belief that the *Palaiapolis,* mentioned in classical sources, was identified with the Medes Islands. The complex Emporitan historiography established the parameters on which modern knowledge is based, especially and in a definitive way, since 1908. The "Junta de Museus de Barcelona" bought the lands and started the systematic archaeological exploration of the remains found in the subsoil in the area of the Neapolis and in the Roman city. This project was guided by the architect Josep Puig i Cadafalch and carried out by Emili Gandia. Since it started, the research has continued without interruption up to the present, with a pause during the Spanish Civil War.

Nowadays, when we talk of Empúries we should bear in mind the different nuclei of the archaeological site that have been incorporated over the years of research into the historic knowledge about the city. Among these the following are worthy of a mention.

a) Sant Martí d'Empúries. The first Greek settlement of *Emporion* was established here, in the second quarter of the 6th century BC, on the site of a previous indigenous village, which must have dated back to the end of the Bronze Age (9th to 8th centuries BC). Once the Greeks had established themselves on terra firma, they referred to this first settlement as the old city (*Palaiapolis*). Of all the Emporitan nuclei, Sant Martí d'Empúries is the only one that has been continuously inhabited until the present. It was the seat of the Late Roman city of Empúries, the Visigothic Episcopal seat, the county capital of Mediaeval Empúries and, in the 16th century, the birthplace of the town of L'Escala.

b) The Neapolis (The new city). This corresponds to the sector of the Greek city of *Emporion* built on terra firma, that was given this name by J. Puig i Cadafalch to distinguish it from the *Palaiapolis*. It was to the south of the port, and over the years it extended from the southern extreme until reaching a maximum area of about four hectares. The archaeological remains make up part of the present itinerary of the site. It should, however, be mentioned that the majority of the visible structures belong to more modern phases in the life of the city (2nd and 1st centuries BC). The previous phases, of Greek chronology, are much less known, and we still do not have all the details on its urbanisation.

c). The Roman city. This was situated on the top of the Emporitan hill. Its foundation, at the beginning of the 1st century BC, was on top of the remains of a Roman military camp installed after the indigenous revolt in 197 BC. The archaeological remains are part of the current itinerary. Although we know the main characteristics of the orthogonal urban layout and the perimeter boundaries, with an area of 22.5 hectares, most of the city has yet to be discovered.

d) The ancient port and the Hellenistic jetty. The ancient natural port was between the *Palaiapolis* and the Neapolis. Now buried, the only visible remains are the breakwater which was built in the Roman Republican period (2nd and 1st centuries BC). Other remains of the

1.- Sant Martí d'Empúries, the ancient *Palaiapolis*, the first Greek settlement founded in the second quarter of the 6ᵗʰ century BC, and later a Late Roman and Mediaeval centre.
2.- The *Emporion polis*, the Greek city established on terra firma in about 550 BC, also known as the Neapolis.
3.- The Roman city, the name of which is unknown, created at the beginning of the 1st century BC in the highest part of the Emporitan hill, based on an earlier Roman military settlement. In Augustan times, it was unified with the Greek city to become the *municipium Emporiae*.
4.- Les Corts hill, to the west of the urban nuclei, used as a cemetery in various phases of the history of Empúries (outside this itinerary)
5.- High Mediaeval churches (outside this itinerary): 5a) Santa Margarida 5b) Santa Magdalena, 5c) Sant Vicenç.
6.- Hellenistic jetty (2ⁿᵈ and 1ˢᵗ centuries BC)

port structures of Empúries can be seen in the Riells-La Clota area, to the south of L'Escala.

e) The suburban and the necropolis areas. Outside the urban boundaries of Empúries hill, limited by the walls, several Greek, indigenous, Roman and Late Roman necropolises have been discovered. In addition, in the car park to the south of the Neapolis are the visible remains of an industrial metallurgic factory. The excavations in this sector were unsuccessful attempts to find the capital of the *indiketes*, the Iberian inhabitants of the area, who were mentioned in classical sources. At present the possible location of this Iberian nucleus is still unknown.

f) The churches of Santa Margarida and Santa Magdalena. These are located on the west slope of the Empúries hill, on either side of the road that leads to Sant Martí. They are part of the different settlements of the Late Roman and High Mediaeval periods, surrounding the city of Empúries.

Aerial view of the whole of the site of Empúries.

g) "Les Corts" hill. Occupied since Neolithic times, it was used as a necropolis area at the end of the Bronze Age (Parrallí necropolis), in Roman Republican times (the "Les Corts" necropolis) and also as a cemetery in the Late Roman period, as can be seen by the remains of a funeral monument from this latter period situated in the highest part. To the south west there are still the High Mediaeval structures of the church of Sant Vicenç.

h) Cinc Claus. In the little village of Cinc Claus, built on a small elevated piece of land to the northwest of the Empúries hill, is the High Mediaeval church of Santa Reparada, possibly built on top of previous structures.

# Pre-colonial Empúries

Recent excavations carried out in different parts of the Emporitan area have offered new data about the occupation in this coastal sector of the Empordan territory before the arrival of the Greeks. Although there is some inconclusive evidence dating back to Neolithic times, the effective beginnings of the settlement belong to the end of the Bronze age, in the 9th to 8th centuries BC. The type of hand-made pottery found at the deepest archaeological levels documented, in the subsoil of the present village of Sant Martí d'Empúries during the excavations since 1994, has been attributed to this cultural phase.

This information shows the existence of a small, relatively stable village community, that occupied a settlement set out in the open air, and one which made the most of the resources around it. Its economy was based on stockbreeding and the agricultural use of the nearby flat areas that were not either ponds or marshes. The strategic placement of this small coastal promontory also permitted other activities, such as on the one hand fishing and collecting molluscs, and on the other hand the chance to maintain the beginning of relationships with the exterior, which were mainly based on trading in metals.

Although we are still not sure as to the exact layout of this first habitat, the information gathered from excavations at other sites around the same cultural time, such as La Fonollera, at the south of the Massis del Montgrí, leads us to believe that there was a small group of rectangular huts, built with a mixture of foliage and mud, reinforced with posts thrust into the ground.

In the Empordan area, the next historic period was the transition from the end of the Bronze age to the Iron Age, a very slow process that took place during the 8th and 7th centuries BC. During this period there were important changes and innovations, motivated on the one hand by the migration of Indo-European population to Catalonia, the people of Urnfields culture, and on the other hand by the contacts that were developing at the end of this time thanks to the commerce with other Mediterranean areas that were culturally more advanced. All these factors favoured the development of these indigenous villages, with cultural manifestations which affected, in a similar way, a wider territory beyond the Empordan region, across the Pyrenees to the plains of Roussillon and Languedoc, known as the Mailhacian culture.

From the earliest years of this period, before 650 BC, several necropolises have been found in the Empordà that show the adoption of cremation as a funeral rite, in which the ashes of the deceased were placed in urns made of clay which were buried together with various objects that made up the funeral goods. Amongst these necropolises are Can Bech de Baix (Agullana), and on

A set of hand-made indigenous pottery, consisting of a lipped cup, decorated with motifs of meanders, and of a *kernos*, or ritual cup, consisting of three receptacles that are joined together, dating to the end of the Bronze age. They were found in the Paralli necropolis, at the western side of les Corts hill.

the outskirts of Empúries, the Parrallí, on the west side of "Les Corts" hill (outside the site of the museum). In contrast, we have discovered few examples of habitats from this period. In the case of the Emporitan area, evidence shows that at that time Sant Martí d'Empúries hill was temporarily abandoned as a habitat, possibly due to a preference for other areas on the plain, slightly more inland, as we can deduce from the location of the site at Parrallí.

After the second half of the 7th century BC, now well into the Iron Age, Sant Martí hill was occupied again, this time by a small indigenous group which would soon become involved with commercial routes crossing the extreme northwest of the Mediterranean, promoted by the Phoenician centres from the south and east of the peninsula, as well as from the Etruscan cities. Without

Reconstruction of the ancient landscape of the area of Empúries. The promontory of Sant Martí, next to the old course of the River Fluvià, was joined to the hill where the Greek and Roman cities would later be built, by a narrow isthmus, creating a small bay which could be used as a natural port (Drawing J. Sagrera).

A hand-made pottery urn belonging to the first Iron Age, from the excavations carried out in the Main Square of Sant Martí d'Empúries. On the right, you can see a detail of a small domestic oven found inside one of the huts.

doubt, being able to take advantage of the possibilities of the nearby coast as a port for this small isle favoured the beginnings of these commercial activities, which from that moment on would promote the later development of the Emporitan settlement. On the other hand, we know that this was not the only settlement in the area, as we have evidence of the existence of other similar settlements that were more closely linked to the plain.

We know some of the characteristics of the domestic constructions in the village established in the higher part of Sant Martí hill. They were roughly rectangular spaces, laid out in lines and limited by walls made of mud and woven foliage, mounted on a small plinth of stones and clay. In some places there are only the remains of the holes into which the support posts for the structure of the huts were placed. Inside, the floors and the fireplaces were made of different layers of hardened clay. Worthy of a mention is the fact that one of the areas has a small domestic circular oven, also made of clay.

The material culture of this settlement mainly consists of hand-made pottery, possibly locally made, but closely based on the types of vases and decorative designs characteristic of the advanced phase of the Mailhacian culture. Amongst the objects made of bronze, there are plenty of items of personal adornment, such as fibulae, buckles for belts, needles, chains, buttons, bracelets and so on. The known necropolises in the Empordan and

graphical references, together with the discovery of archaeological material from the archaic period, enabled this place to be rapidly identified as Sant Martí d'Empúries. This model of foundation (establishing a settlement on a small island close to the coast thereby offering a greater degree of security) was well known in the Greek colonial world and there are other examples in the Mediterranean. The main aim was to have a stopover and supporting port rather than to create a centre from which to intervene directly on the immediate territory. Neither was it at all surprising that at that time the place was already occupied by a small indigenous community, as we saw in the previous chapter.

*Lidion* vase made in Eastern Greece, decorated with painted bands, from Empúries, preserved in the Museu d'Arqueologia de Catalunya-Barcelona (575-550 BC).

Recent archaeological digs in the nucleus of Sant Martí have shown that between the end of the 7th century BC and the beginning of the 6th, together with the Phoenician and Etruscan imports, some pottery started to arrive from Greece, although still in small quantities, in particular from Corinth and above all from Ionia. Without doubt this can be considered a result of the founding of *Massalia* and of the first Phocaean entry into the commercial routes already established in that part of the northwest Mediterranean. The effective establishment of a commercial factory, the origin of the Greek city of *Emporion*, occurred a few decades later. From the second quarter of the 6th century BC the volume of imports, as far as archaeological finds are concerned, increased significantly, and at the same time the corresponding proportion of indigenous materials decreased. Pottery of Etruscan origin, particularly amphorae, still represented an important percentage of the imports. However, the strong presence of Western Greek products, above all those that originated from *Massalia,* is a clear indication of the close links between the first Emporitan settlement and this city.

**20**

The remains of the domestic constructions from this period found during the digs in the "Plaça Major" (the Main Square) of Sant Martí, also show significant changes that must be related to the Phocaean presence in the area. Although the information available is scarce, this

The remains of a relief sculpted in sandstone, representing sphinxes. It came from the *Palaiapolis*. It must have belonged to the frieze of a temple, maybe that of Artemis of Ephesus. The original is in the Museu d'Arqueologia de Catalunya-Barcelona.

archaic habitat, dating from just before the middle of the 6th century BC, shows a type of construction that is more solid than the indigenous huts of the previous period. There were rectangular rooms, limited by walls made of mud bricks and plinths made of stones bonded together with clay. The fireplaces, which were circular, were made of a layer of clay on top of a base support of small stones and fragments of pottery. In other sectors of the hill there is evidence of traditional activities, already developed in this archaic period, such as bronze metallurgy or pottery-making in a clearly Ionian way.

Very probably, the presence of the first Phocaean or Marseilles traders did not mean that the place was abandoned by the indigenous people, and they must have coexisted in peace, given the interests of both communities. The small area of the place and, consequently, the

A Greek zoomorphic vase (*askos*) in the shape of a horse (6th century), possibly from the excavations of the Greek necropolis "El Portixol".

reduced number of newly arrived settlers, doubtless limited its ability to influence. However, excavations have also offered evidence of the social, economic and cultural transformation of these indigenous communities, which was, on the whole, favoured by these contacts, through trade with more advanced cultures. Firstly, with traders of Phoenician and Etruscan origin and finally, and in a more direct way, with the Greeks who settled in the territory. This transformation process determined the development of a  whole series of new cultural features which were to define what is known as the Iberian culture, which covered a great part of the coast of the far west of the Mediterranean. Written sources have enabled us to know the name of the native ethnic group that occupied the Empordan territory, the "indigetes". These were the people with whom the first Greeks to settle in Empúries made contact. Archaeological finds recovered from the excavations show some important technological innovations in the material of indigenous tradition, such as the beginnings of making pottery with a wheel or a greater presence of metal tools and objects.

The relationship between the Greeks and the local population must have been a satisfactory one, and evidence of this is the establishing, a few years later, of the new city on terra firma. Despite this, life and activity on the ancient *Palaiapolis* continued in strength. In fact, from the end of the 6th century BC and throughout the 5th century there is documentation of an important urban restructuring on the north slope of Sant Martí hill. The houses were aligned on either side of streets that were perfectly adapted to the irregular topography of the land. In one way or another occupation of the small coastal hill would continue in later periods and right up to the present. Further on, we will talk about the vicissitudes of the village in later periods.

Finally, we would like to mention a quote from Strabon, according to which the Emporitans worshipped Artemis of Ephesus, one of the Phocaean national goddesses. We have not yet found a temple dedicated to her worship in the ancient *Palaiapolis*, although it is assumed that, should it have existed, it would be under the present site of the church, inferring that this area has been used for purposes of worship right up to the present. The existence of ancient architectural elements that make up part of its foundations could corroborate this hypothesis. It would seem that the discovery of a fragment of sculpted frieze with the representation of two sphinxes, at the beginning of the century, is another bit of evidence that this temple existed. A huge capital made of sandstone with scrolls at the corners indicates that the style would have been Ionian.

We also know some of the areas where the first Greeks to arrive at Empúries used to bury their dead, such as the "El Portixol" necropolis, to the south-east of the Neapolis, just next to the present-day Hotel Ampurias. Despite the fact that the area suffered from systematic plundering and was also partially destroyed at the end of the last century by the road that follows the coastline, some material has been recovered, and its dating leads us to believe that it did in fact correspond to the cemetery used by the Greeks during this first phase. Unlike the indigenous necropolises, the dominant funeral rite here was burial.

# The city on terra firma:
# the Neapolis

Within a short time, the limitations of the *Palaiapolis* and the strengthening of contacts with the native population must have meant that it was advisable to move to terra firma. This new nucleus, which we know as the Neapolis, is just south of the village of Sant Martí, next to the natural shelter converted into a port. The excavations that started in 1908 revealed almost all the structures that correspond to this later phase of occupation, now fully Roman. It should be taken into consideration during your visit that the level of this area is appreciably higher than the level of the ancient Greek town. This continuity of

occupation is what led to the vertical development, meaning that in the areas which have been excavated to a greater depth there are still walls and buildings from previous times that are visible. Excavations in the Neapolis have allowed us to establish, *grosso modo,* that the founding of this new nucleus was towards the middle of the 6th century BC. This was a time when important events were occurring in the Mediterranean, and the Emporitan colony could not be separated. We should remember that the fall of Phocaea to the Persians happened in 540 BC, just five years before the defeat of Alalia, and that this must have caused a significant exodus to the westernmost colonies, especially Marseilles, that from this time on was to become an authentic metropolis.

The word Neapolis, which we use for this Greek nucleus established on terra firma, was created by Puig i Cadafalch, the first director of the Emporitan archaeological excavations, to contrast it with the *Palaiapolis* (the old city) mentioned in the sources that referred to the first settlement at Sant Martí. Despite the intense scientific

Attic jug in the shape of a female head, found in tomb number 19 of the Martí necropolis, between the Greek and Roman nuclei. (450 BC)

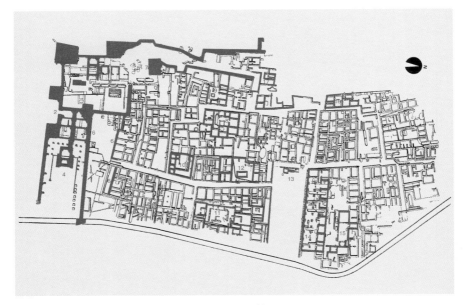

General plan of the Neapolis and the main points of interest.

Containers for perfumes (*alabastron* and *lekitos*) made of Attic pottery in the black-figure style, from funeral goods (6th century BC)

activity that has been carried out since 1908, we are aware that our knowledge about the Greek city of Empúries is, as will be seen shortly, rather limited. It is true that the spectacular discovery of the statue of Asclepius in 1909 created an increased interest in the excavations of the site, so that work continued without interruption until the beginning of the Spanish Civil War in 1936. The amount of earth that was removed by the first excavators must have been considerable, especially if we consider that dunes and cultivated land completely covered the remains of the city, as can be seen in some of the old photos and postcards that reflect the state of the site at the beginning of the century. This work affected the whole of the remains that make up the Neapolis, in varying degrees. In the southern sector and above all in the area around the edicule of Asclepius, due to the discovery of the image of this god, they excavated right down to the lowest levels, to just above the rock, whilst in other areas of the city they simply uncovered the levels

Detail of a Greek house, excavated in the far north of the Neapolis.

and remains of buildings that corresponded to the later phase of occupation. On the whole, the research affected buildings and areas of a public nature, such as the agora and the stoa, the main streets, the religious area and part of the defence walls of the city.

Later, in the forties, archaeological activity in the Neapolis concentrated only on specific investigations in order to obtain a stratigraphic sequence of the development of the site from its beginnings through to its final abandonment. After 1985, and after a long period of inactivity in the Greek city, a series of campaigns were started, aimed at researching mainly the religious area situated in the southern sector. The main objective of this work was to establish more precisely the chronology of the different buildings and therefore to determine the development and transformations that occurred over time. The results obtained in the study of this sector enable us to propose, thanks to the relevance and significance of the buildings, an approximation of the general development of the *Emporion* city.

The current state of research does not allow us to be more precise about the characteristics of the Greek *polis* in the middle of the 6$^{th}$ century BC. The chronology of the different parts of the walls that have been discovered so far lead us to believe that the growth of the city occurred mainly to the south. At the moment, the oldest and best-known defence wall corresponds to an extension that

Attic column crater in the red-figure style, on which you can see a funeral scene. On one side, you can see three young people, dressed in tunics (*himation*), one of whom is offering a drink as a farewell gesture. On the other side the deceased, who is drunk, is going to the other world to the sound of a flute, whilst a friend is trying to retain him (460-450 BC)

Details of the decoration of the Attic crater with red-figures and the representation of the funeral scene.

was built in the 4th century BC, and therefore we are unaware of the size of the original nucleus, although we imagine it must have been slightly smaller. According to the stratigraphic data obtained from different excavations, the oldest levels documented to date are situated precisely in the areas near the low-lying area that was used as a port, between the present-day Sant Martí d'Empúries and the Greek city.

Jug with a three-lobular lip made of *bucchero nero* Etruscan pottery. These were imported materials that made up part of the funeral goods in the indigenous necropolis of the Northeast Wall (4th century BC).

Although we cannot say much about the urban structure during this period, it is possible to offer a few ideas. The first is that it must have been conditioned by the topographical features of the land on which it was built. The Neapolis, which covered a total area of about four hectares, was dominated by a rocky outcrop called Torre Talaia, to the far west. Excavations in this area seem to confirm that it was occupied well into the past, which would seem logical considering that the rest of the city was dominated by this point. A lack of more extensive excavations mean that we must assume that right from the very first moment, this area made up part of the walled area of the Greek *polis*. The remains of a tower framework from the beginning of the 5th century BC and other walls of an equally defensive appearance, that form a kind of acropolis in this sector would seem to confirm this hypothesis. There are just a few blocks of calcareous stone remaining of the tower, which made up the southwest angle, built onto the natural rock. This structu-

Iberian stele made of sandstone, of uncertain origin. This block, which was rectangular with the top part rounded off, was decorated symmetrically on both sides. The design can be interpreted as a rolled up lance ending in a triangular point, leading us to believe that is was the stele of a warrior, who once dead had been buried with all his equipment (6th century BC).

re was modified or rebuilt during the 2nd century BC. The results of the excavations in the southern sector of the Neapolis also lead us to believe that, under the shelter of the Greek nucleus, there was a quarter that was outside the city walls, possibly inhabited by the indigenous people who, as time went by and their relationship with the Greeks improved, decided to settle in the surrounding areas of *Emporion*. Classical sources tell us about the relationship between the two ethnic peoples, and confirm that originally the Greeks were physically separated from the indigenous people by a wall. However, it is impossible to imagine that a permanent situation of mistrust existed, especially if we consider the common interests they shared. On the one hand the Greeks needed the land for their own survival, whilst the dynamic role the Phocaean colony played on the indigenous population is indubitable, and helped in shaping the particular characteristics of the Iberian culture in the area. We do not yet know the general characteristics of this nucleus situated outside *Emporion*: We do know that the people lived in houses that, thanks to the materials used in their construction, were very similar to those documented inside the Greek city. The walls were made of a stone plinth about fifty centimetres high on which they put mud bricks dried in the sun. The flooring inside the houses was flattened mud and inside there were often remains of small domestic stoves or small silos for storing grain or other provisions. Rather than thinking of a settlement with a specific organisation similar to other Iberian villages, it is probably more accurate to imagine this as a quarter that just grew up over time, without there necessarily having been any express wish for it to become anything else.

The existence of separate cemeteries is another piece of evidence that originally the two communities occupied clearly different areas which were governed by different sets of rules. If we look back at the Emporitan necropolises corresponding to the 6th and 5th centuries BC, we can see that the cultural goods, the cinerary urns and the rest of elements that made up the funeral goods show this. We have discovered about twenty tombs in the necropo-

A funeral set from the excavations in tomb number 11 of the necropolis of the Northeast Wall, which was a cremation cemetery to the west of the ancient port, which must have corresponded to the indigenous population installed around Empúries. It consists of an urn with a lid and other hand-made pottery cups, bronze objects, an iron knife and a faience scarab from the Greek colony of *Naukratis* in Egypt (6th century BC).

lis at the Northeast Wall, most of which were cremations. The links with the indigenous community is shown thanks to the presence of a large quantity of pieces of hand-made pottery, especially the urns that contained the ashes, which are similar to those discovered in other native cemeteries. Despite the great preponderance of locally made material, imported pottery has also been documented, such as Etruscan cups and jugs of *bucchero nero,* pottery from Attica and Corinth, and so on. The appearance of metal objects, such as fragments of iron daggers and bronze spherical helmets, leads us to believe that some of these tombs belonged to warriors. The dating of this necropolis, between the second half of the 6th century BC and the first half of the 5th, indicate that this must have been one of the burial areas used by the indigenous community which, as we have already said, must have installed themselves around *Emporion.*

On the other hand, we also know about other cemeteries that, due to the material used to make up the funeral goods, and the rituals used, are related to the Greek city of *Emporion.* The most important of these is the Bonjoan necropolis to the south of the Neapolis, very close to the present car park. The sizes of these cemeteries are hard to estimate as their use often goes beyond a specific period, as we have seen from the recent excavations in the car park, where on lower levels (which cannot now be seen) we discovered a first phase corresponding to a necropolis from the 4th and 3rd centuries, which possibly later formed part of the Bonjoan cemetery. However, more detailed study of the tombs seems to indicate that the oldest ones, from the second half of the 6th century and the 5th century BC, mainly burials, were the ones that were the furthest away, which confirms the previous idea.

## The city defences

The urban development and growth of the Greek city, over the years, led to important changes both in its appearance and in its organisation and internal structure. Of these changes, the ones which affected the defence limits of the city are especially significant. The study of these great public works allows us to know more about determined aspects of the history of the Greek *Emporion*, such as the different large phases of the growth and urban expansion, the characteristics of the defence structures or the techniques they used for cutting the stone. The superimposition of the structures and the vertical growth in the Greek city make studying lower levels very difficult. However, work that has been carried out over recent years in the southern sector of the Neapolis has yielded some information and led to new hypotheses about some of the historical mysteries that were being investigated.

Traditionally, it was believed that the walls where today's visit to the site starts, were the ones that surrounded the Greek *polis* right from the start. This hypothesis, in turn, had conditioned the global interpretation of the development of the site. Its dating towards the middle of the 2nd century BC meant that the defences corresponding to the previous period had to be sought. They were eventually found about twenty-five metres further north. This previous wall was about two metres in width, with a cyclopean appearance, and built of a double face of ashlars which was lined with stones and earth inside. It is preserved unevenly, the eastern end being the highest,

**6**

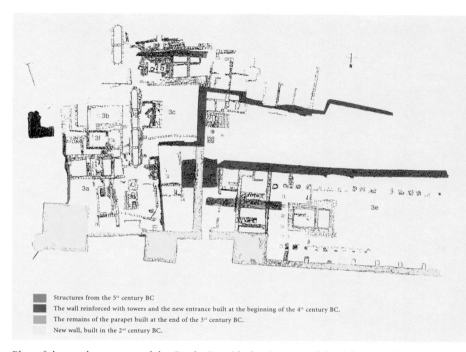

Structures from the 5ᵗʰ century BC

The wall reinforced with towers and the new entrance built at the beginning of the 4ᵗʰ century BC.

The remains of the parapet built at the end of the 3ʳᵈ century BC.

New wall, built in the 2ⁿᵈ century BC.

Plan of the southern sector of the Greek city with the situation of the defence walls.

at about three metres, and its whole length lies on natural rock. It corresponds to a extension of the urban perimeter built during the first half of the 4ᵗʰ century BC, and meant the destruction of some of the buildings that were

Detail of the excavation to the road that led into the Neapolis. In the background you can see one of the towers to reinforce the southern wall of *Emporion* which dates back to the beginning of the 4ᵗʰ century BC.

Hypothetical reconstruction of the southern wall of the Greek city (4th century BC).

to the south of the Greek nucleus. It was reinforced by two solid, quadrangular towers, also made of stone, of which we have only recovered the remains that correspond to the foundations. In the far east, just where nowadays there is the promenade that follows the coastline, a bastion of large dimensions has been found, which was probably built to reinforce this part from a defensive point of view.

Access to the inside of the urban nucleus was in the far west, partly making use of the remains of a huge podium built before the above-mentioned extension in the 4th

century BC, which together with one of the towers formed a passage that communicated with the inner square, from where the city itself could be reached. The total
size of the urban site is hard to say, especially if we consider that the continuation of this wall can only be followed along the west side, whilst on the east side its layout
is still unknown to us. These defences were partially
dismantled both in Antiquity and later to make use of
the materials in other buildings. For example, in the
rebuilding of the walls in the middle of the 2nd century
BC or for building the convent for the Servite monks in
the 17th century.

The existence of a sanctuary dedicated to Asclepius, the
Greek god of medicine, is evident thanks to the discovery
of a statue of this god during the excavation works in
1909. The statue was dumped into a cistern just in front
of an edicule that was framed with huge blocks of calcareous rocks, where we assume the image must have
been placed. This little temple was built just after the
remodelling of the city walls at the beginning of the 4th
century BC, and marked the beginning of the configuration of a religious complex that lasted until the end of
*Emporion* itself.

However, the excavations have allowed us to recover
some of the architectural elements of a temple prior to
that of Asclepius, which was much larger, and about
which, unfortunately, we have no idea as to the god to
whom it was dedicated. We only know a little about the
roof, which was made of stone tiles finished off with antefixes made of sedimentary stone which were decorated
with palmettes and lotus flowers alternately. The acroterium that crowned the upper part of the pediment was
made out of the same material and its decoration has
been reconstructed from just three tiny fragments. The
concentration of all these finds around the area of the
sanctuary to Asclepius and the fact that some of them
were found just below the foundations lead us to believe
that this must have been the first temple raised in this
sector. The lack of information we have about the actual

## The area of the sanctuaries: the worship of Asclepius.

3a

The statue of Asclepius, the Greek god of medicine, which was found in Empúries and is currently on display at the Museu d'Arqueologia de Catalunya -Barcelona. It is larger than life size, and is made of two different marbles, one from the island of Paros and the other from Attican Pentelic quarries. He is wearing a tunic and sandals. His left hand was leaning on a staff, and in his right hand he held a patera. The style and the technique used show that the piece was made at the end of the 4<sup>th</sup> century BC. Over time it was repaired, as can be seen by parts of the snake made of pieces of local sandstone.

limits of the Greek city during the 5<sup>th</sup> century BC makes it very difficult to interpret this monument although it would seem that it was built outside the perimeter that was surrounded by the walls, with the aim of it becoming a place of common worship for Greeks and indigenous people, thus fostering and increasing the ties between both races.

We do not know, either, the reasons for which it was dismantled in the 4<sup>th</sup> century BC, although possibly it could be related to the process of fusion that led to the extension of the city walls to the south, so as to include in the site itself the nucleus that had been growing up around the Greek *polis* since its founding. The rebuilding of this

Aerial view of the sector of the sanctuaries in the Greek city.

sector meant that from that time on, there was an area  that was perfectly limited and with a clear religious purpose. The worship area was organised around the temple to Asclepius, in the highest sector and in a dominant position. We know that part of this corresponded to the base, made of huge blocks of square calcareous stone, as well as the remains of the mosaic flooring from the most recent times of its use. This podium is divided internally by a wall that separates the rear part the *cella,* where the image of the god was placed, from the *pronaos,* or entrance area, which was made up of a portico with two lateral and four front columns. Access to the temple must have been by means of stairs at the front, which have disappeared due to later reforms.

This religious complex was completed by an altar, just in front of the temple to Asclepius, which was a raised platform that could be reached by means of a small outside staircase. Further to the south there is also another altar crowned by two identical altar stones, and bounded at

A photograph showing the moment when part of the statue of Asclepius was found in 1909, inside one of the compartments of the large cistern just in front of the temple.

The podium of the temple to Asclepius made of blocks of local calcareous stone. Behind this is the *cella* where the image of the deity was on view.

Piece of sedimentary stone that was part of the architectural decoration of a temple built in the southern sector of the Greek city during the 5$^{th}$ century BC. It was one of the antefixes that was part of the eaves of the roof. The front is decorated with a palmette. On the back there is a Greek letter, which served as a number, which must have been to identify where it was to be placed.

least on the west side, by a flight of steps. The existence of a cistern situated at the foot of the temple to Asclepius is interesting in connection with the worship ritual, since this cistern must have provided the water required for the cures or ablution rituals for the sick people who visited the sanctuary. The importance of this cistern is evident in successive changes that were made in order to adapt it to the transformations that affected the *Asklepieion* and to prevent the progressive raising of the level of the floor from putting it out of use. Water was an essential element in the curing rituals and was used to purify the body of the sick person. These people could also be put through the stages of incubus or sacred sleep when the god gave the necessary advice for the faithful. The excavation of the areas next to the temple to Asclepius has allowed us to recover different votive vases and some *ex votos* offered for the sick who, once they had recovered, made sacrifices and offerings to the god. Despite the fact that this edicule would remain the centre of the worship centre, the aspect and organisation of the sanctuary were remodelled in a significant way in the middle of the 2nd century BC coinciding, yet again, with the extension towards the south of the city perimeter.

## The Greek necropolises

The particular Emporitan topography, with a large amount of high areas and small hills surrounded by an extensive marsh area, conditioned not only the distribution of the inhabited areas, but also that of the cemeteries. Their excavation was carried out mainly after the forties with the aim of putting an end to the long spell of plundering of many of the tombs and to prevent the dispersion of the objects and works of art. The global study of these necropolises was to become yet another element for completing the reconstruction and development of the live city, at the same time offering information about the customs and funeral rites of their inhabitants. In Greek *Emporion* the dominant ritual was inhumation. The body, with its head facing east, was placed inside a very simple grave dug out of the soil itself or in the natural rock. Sometimes the grave was defined by a row of stones. Goods were placed in the grave with the deceased person, such as objects denoting their social presti-

Structures corresponding to a pedestal of double altar stones, at the south of the temple to Asclepius (4th century BC).

Containers for ointments and perfumes, made out of different coloured core-formed glass. They were made in the eastern area of the Mediterranean, and were often found in Emporitan funeral goods in the 5th century BC.

ge, personal possessions or those related to the activity the person had carried out during their life. There were also ritual vessels for potions and ointments, as well as pieces of pottery that must have contained food for the journey ahead. Often there were imported objects, which allow us to date the grave precisely, such as Attic vessels decorated with black and red figures or ointment containers of core-formed glass.

Previously, we mentioned the burial areas where the oldest tombs were documented. Amongst the necropolises in Greek tradition that we know about, the oldest is "El Portixol", to the south of the Neapolis. Despite there being little documentation about it, thanks to the material preserved we can date it to the 6th century BC. Therefore, its use can be associated with the first Greeks who settled in Empúries. On the other hand the native population would have used, at the same time, other different burial grounds, such as the so-called necropolis of the Northeast Wall, where the funeral rites used were almost exclusively cremation.

As we have already mentioned, the study of the Emporitan necropolises (which cannot be visited) is an indication of the development of *Emporion*. Therefore, after the unification process between the indigenous and the Greek communities, that we relate to the extension of

A terracotta figure representing an ithyphallic Hermes, which was part of the funeral goods of burial tomb number 20 of the Martí necropolis.

Attic jugs decorated with black figures, from tomb number 164 of the Bonjoan necropolis (second half of the 6th century BC)

Terracotta figure showing a reclining male at a banquet. In his left hand he is holding a cup or *kylix*. This was found in the excavation of the Greek tomb number 77 of the Martí necropolis (5th century BC).

the defensive perimeters at the beginning of the 4th century BC, it is logical to imagine that the burial areas would have been shared. This is how we interpret the necropolises that occupy a large part of the southern area of the Emporitan hill, known as the Bonjoan and the Car Park necropolises where, after the oldest phase (since the 6th century BC) which is characterised by the exclusive use of inhumation, there is evidence of the combination of the two rituals, reflecting the new Emporitan reality. Finally, we should mention one of the Greek necropolises that was still used in the more recent periods, known as the Martí cemetery. This is situated to the north of the strip there is between the Greek and the Roman cities, in which, apart from showing the dual funeral practices, we can deduce, due to the presence of imported Italic objects, the beginning of the third element, the Roman one, which was to shape the new Empúries.

Of all the reasons that motivated the arrival of the Greek sailors at our coasts, probably the most important was that of founding a chain of ports in order to establish a commercial route that would reach the far west of the Mediterranean. The main commercial routes were established with the south of the peninsula that was under Punic influence, with Ibiza, with the Phocaean world and finally with the indigenous people. The name they gave the city – *Emporion* – which in Greek means market, shows yet again this commercial vocation. In the same way, the model followed by the creation of this enclave shows, by setting up on a kind of island, at least during the initial phase, the desire for a stopover port rather than the firm decision to exploit local resources. Soon, however, and after a period of initial trial and error, the small nucleus extended to terra firma. From that moment on, the Emporitan intervention in the immediate territory must have been very decisive, as is shown by the urban development and expansion of *Emporion* itself and the majority of the indigenous villages in the surrounding area.

## Economy and commerce

An amphora from Marseilles for transporting wine (4th century BC). The presence of pottery and other objects from Marseilles and its area of influence was a constant occurrence in Greek *Emporion* of the classical era.

A commercial letter from the 5th century BC, written in Greek, with the letters engraved on a sheet of lead, which was then rolled up and sent. It is written in the Ionian dialect and is from a Phocaean trader giving a series of orders to his representative in *Emporion*.

Although this location offered inferior port conditions to the northern side of the Bay of Roses, which is much more sheltered from the wind, this was compensated by the ease in communication with the interior lands. We should not forget that, despite the fact that the commerce was done via the sea, the redistribution of the products was done by means of small craft which could reach the different villages of the interior along the River Ter, to the south, and Fluvià to the north. The location of *Emporion*, in this sense, was unbeatable. It was right at the mouth of both rivers, meaning that it could act as a centre for delivering the manufactured goods and at the same time channelling the movement of raw materials. Without doubt, this trade generated a class of rich and powerful men who must have had an important influence on the governing of the city.

Greek cities were closely linked to their territory, the *chorá,* and exploited its natural resources, which they used for their own consumption and for export. In the case of *Emporion*, it is difficult to decide whether or not there was a defined territory, precisely delimited and under the direct control of the city. The particular characteristics of the Empordan countryside, dominated by areas of marshes, and the later changes as a result of its drying up, make it difficult to make conclusions about the previous phases. A clear example of these changes is the deviation in the river courses: The Ter, which used to flow out to the south of the city, now does so on the other side of the Massis del Montgrí, and the Fluvià a little to the north of its ancient course. Despite references by some classic sources, such as Strabon (1st century BC), the geographer, or Apianus, the historian (2nd century AD) who mentioned the products the Emporitans exploited and the existence of other nuclei around *Emporion*, we have not been able to find any other evidence to show the existence of a *chorá*. In fact, according to the ideas mentioned earlier, it seems fairly unlikely that during its initial phases the city was capable of directly controlling the territory, above all if we take into consideration that this was not an essential element for the existence of *emporia* or enclaves of these characteristics. It is for this purpose, rather than as an area of exploitation, that the Emporitan *chorá* probably should be interpreted as the area in which the city exercised a more direct influence.

If it is hard to evaluate the role of *Emporion* during the phases just after its founding, it is even harder to be more precise about which products were commercialised. The existence of large fields of silos for grain, around the indigenous villages, which must have served as centres for collecting and storing, lead us to suppose that the object of the commerce was cereal production. However, the information obtained from archaeological research does not allow us to evaluate quantitatively the scope of this trade. Although it is obvious that the function of *Emporion* contributed in a decisive way to the development of the indigenous communities and accelerated the historic process known as "Iberisation". Neither must we forget the exploitation of other materials such as flax and esparto, which are characteristic of marshy areas and which are mentioned in classical texts. Metallurgy (lead, iron or silver) must have been an important activity, as can be shown by the discovery of an industrial complex, although probably dated somewhat later, which is under the present-day car park of the Empúries site. The cultural material which has appeared in some of the villages shows that pottery must have been one of the elements used in interchanges.

Numismatics also offers us some interesting information about the economic history of the Emporitan port and the commercial routes to which it was linked. We know that during the 5th century BC small silver coins were circulating in *Emporion*, with very similar characteristics to the Phocaean ones, possibly originating from *Massalia*. Towards the second half of that same century the city was minting its own silver coins, which were small and without an inscription. They had different symbols (for example the representation of a sheep's head on the front). Later on, and until well into the 4th century BC, this

Emporitan drachma. These silver coins were minted in *Emporion* from the end of the 4th century BC and were the model for indigenous issues. The first minting, influenced by the example of other coins from the Punic area, showed the head of Persephone on the front, with an ear of corn in her hair and the word EMΠOPITΩN (of the Emporitans), and on the back a standing horse crowned by a winged Nike. After the First Punic War, the horse was substituted for Pegasus, who was to become the symbol of the city in later Emporitan minting, and Persephone's head was substituted for that of Arethusa of Syracuse, surrounded by three dolphins.

minting developed into other models, some of which bore the inscription EM, the abbreviation for the name of the city. The designs that appear on these coins often copy those of other issues of Greek origin or from the south of Italy, and particularly the coins from Athens, with the head of Athena on the front and an owl on the back.

It was not until the end of the 4th century BC that the city started to mint silver coins of a greater value, the so-called drachmas, with a weight equivalent to 4.7gr. Strangely, the symbols on these first Emporitan drachmas (the head of Persephone with ears of corn on the front, and a standing horse crowned by a winged Nike on the back), is a clear imitation of the designs that are known from some Punic mints, showing the links that still existed between the city and the Carthaginian commercial area of influence at that time.

Later the standing horse was substituted for the figure of Pegasus, and Persephone's head by the nymph Arethusa, surrounded by three dolphins. This change did not take place until towards the end of the First Punic War. When at the end of the 3rd century BC the armed conflict between the Romans and the Carthaginians restarted, the Emporitan mint issued numerous drachmas, possibly with the aim of contributing to the financing of the expenses occurred due to the presence of the Roman army in the peninsula, as the fact that the weight of these drachmas is close to the metrology of the Roman denarius would seem to indicate. The disappearance of the Greek mintings happened at about the beginning of the 2nd century BC and coincided with the appearance of the first bronze coins with the Iberian inscription UNDIKESKEN (of the indigets) and Roman metrology. These issues continued for the rest of the Late Republican period, adapting their weight to the variations in metrology of Roman bronze coins. The symbology used from this time by the Emporitan mint, preserves on the back the traditional Pegasus design, whilst the front of the as shows a feminine head with a Corinthian helmet (*Pallas Athena*). These motifs were to appear later in Emporitan coins of the Imperial period that gave the Latin name of the city.

# *Emporion* in the context of the Punic Wars and the arrival of the Romans

The last walls built in the Neapolis, seen from the south (2$^{nd}$ century BC).

In previous chapters we have described the evolution of the old Phocaean colony at *Emporion*, from its founding until the stages of urban growth and reform in the 4$^{th}$ century BC. One of the events that was to shape its history was the contact made with Rome during the Punic Wars, when the Romans fought against the Carthaginians for control of the Mediterranean. In this context we must locate the building of the new defensive reinforcement towards the last third of the 3$^{rd}$ century BC in front of the ancient city walls. This was a huge wall, about two metres wide, designed to make attacks difficult for the assault machines, such as battering rams, catapults, and towers, which were greatly developed during the Hellenistic period. With this wall the Emporitans hoped to incorporate into their defence system the necessary

Remains of the parapet or *proteichisma*, built towards the end of the 3$^{rd}$ century BC to reinforce the ancient city walls.

improvements to counteract the danger of the new war tactics, in a moment of insecurity due to the advance of Hannibal's troops on the way to Rome.

The confrontation between the Romans and the Carthaginians was an ancient one. Despite the existence of treaties that clearly delimited the areas of respective influence, which had been defined since 226 BC at the River Ebro, the conflict was not resolved until the final defeat of Carthage. The fear in the Greek colonies in the west of the Mediterranean, including *Emporion*, due to the increase of the area of Carthaginian influence motivated them to ask the Romans for help. The siege of the city of Sagunt provoked the conflict known as the Second Punic War.

We must place the arrival of the Roman troops, under Gnaeus Cornelius Scipio, at the Emporitan port in 218 BC in this framework. Their aim was to cut off the rearguard of Hannibal's army that was marching to Italy. From that moment on Empúries became the gate way for the "Romanisation" of Spain. The most important difference from what the Greek colonisation had meant was that the changes were now very profound and traumatic and mid-term they led to the disappearance of the traditional lifestyle of the indigenous community. In fact, during the previous centuries the relationship between these people and the Greeks at *Emporion* had been, on the whole, derived from commercial activity, and despite their decisive role in the emergence of Iberian culture, the founding of the Phocaean colony did not substantially change the structure and configuration of the territory.

Once the confrontation between the Romans and the Carthaginians was over, the Romans became the hegemonic power, which in a short time would completely dominate the Mediterranean. *Emporion* intervened decisively in this process, at least in the initial phase, as a entry point to the Iberian peninsula for Rome, as can be seen by the use of the port for disembarking troops, first those of Scipio, and then years later, those of the consul

Black glaze pottery made in the Italian peninsula, frequently imported in the 2nd and 1st centuries BC, which accompanied the cargos of wine amphorae, transported in the boats that arrived at the Emporitan port.

Detail of the entrance to the Greek city, built in about 150 BC.

Marcus Porcius Cato, who arrived to crush the indigenous revolt, and thus start the effective military dominance of the territory which, in our case, is shown by the installation of a camp at the highest part of Empúries hill. As some of the chroniclers of the time wrote about these events, the Roman victory was resounding and exemplary. And in fact, from this moment on, indigenous opposition disappeared for once and for all in the Emporitan territory.

The outcome of this conflict must have caused some problems in the Greek city. We must remember that the inclusion of the indigenous population within the city was a fact that can probably be dated back to the 4th century BC, as the results of the excavations to the southern area of the Neapolis would seem to indicate. Despite this apparent contradiction, *Emporion* was a firm ally of Rome at the beginning of the 2nd century BC. The urban reforms carried out make it clear that the economic activity went through one of its most active phases, thanks mainly to the importance of the Emporitan port on the commercial routes from Italy to Hispania. We can suppose that during this time *Emporion* was relatively independent politically, even though they were under Rome, and this was the way to pay for the support they had given to the cause. This is the historic context in which we must understand the urban changes that will be mentioned next.

## The city walls and the reforms in the religious area

As from the first half of the 2nd century BC, the Greek city started the remodelling of the walls that made up its southern limit. These important works did not involve an increase in the residential area, but in the religious area that had been established in this sector almost since *Emporion* was founded. By moving the defence limits 25 metres to the south, they created an area suitable for building the new constructions that would complete, at least at that time, the religious complex dedicated to Asclepius.

This reform involved dismantling the wall and the towers built in the first half of the 4th century BC, both the part that is visible and the foundations. With this work the builders recovered a great quantity of the stone ashlars that were later used in the construction of the new walls. This explains its archaic aspect, which is why it was previously considered to be older than in fact it is. Roughly half way along this wall there was the entrance gate to the city, that as we can see from the vertical grooves on the lateral blocks, could be closed to the outside by means of a gate made of iron bars. This entrance also had a second wooden door, with a double swing, of which we still have the two hinges, which were covered in lead. On the outside access was protected by two symmetric towers which were almost square and built of large blocks of calcareous stone, although the upper part, which was covered, was made of other material. Further to the west there is a third larger tower which used the outcrops of rock as a base and which was to protect the south-east corner, where the wall changed direction and headed towards the north.

The gateway in the wall led to a narrow passage limited to the west by a large wall which separated the street from the upper terrace, and to the east by three consecutive rooms. During the excavations the remains of the mechanism of a small crossbow and iron arrow heads were recovered, as well as a large number of lead projectiles, leading us to believe that these rooms were for the guards who had to watch over the entrance to the inside of the city. At the end of the entrance passage

**2**

Amphora used for transporting Italic wine, one of the products that made up the intense trading in the Mediterranean in the 2nd and 1st centuries BC.

there is a second door, of which only the foundation remains, which communicated with a square that was the meeting place between the high terrace and the low one and from where the visit can be continued following the main street going north to south. The reforms also meant an increase in the floor level in the whole of this sector, which from this time onwards was organised into three artificial terraces descending towards the sea. Communication between the three levels was by means of the intermediate terrace, which corresponded to the square situated just beyond the entrance passage to the city and from which, by means of stairs, they could reach the upper or lower terraces.

In the highest and most dominant part of this sector there was the temple to Asclepius, the origin of which dates back to the 4th century. Modifications made to this area were not that important, as is seen by the survival of the altar just in front of Asclepius' podium as well as the double stone altar. We can only confirm a raise in the floor level in the square, shown on the threshold of the new entrance door. The great wall which delimited the entrance street from the city to the west also served as a retention wall for the earth of this higher terrace. The difference in height was made good by means of a small stairway made from blocks of sandstone, which are not currently visible due to the reforms that were carried out at a later date.

The work carried out on the lower terrace was of a much greater magnitude. Here they must have brought in a considerable amount of earth in order to achieve a flat level. This filling in, which in some areas is over two metres deep, meant that they covered a good part of the structures from the previous phase, such as the *proteichisma* or the reinforced wall built in the 3rd century BC, and part of the *vallum* or moat that was in front of it, in such a way that the new walls were also the foundations of the retention walls. There is a large rectangle of about 50 metres in length by 25 in width, surrounded by a portico, of which the base, the capitals and the shafts of some columns allow us to reconstruct the aspect this

Bi-conical jug and patera made of the so-called Emporitan grey pottery, one of the productions that was widely spread in the northeastern area of the Iberian peninsula (2$^{nd}$ and 1$^{st}$ centuries BC).

square must have had. The small portico in the west wing should be mentioned for its uniqueness, which is double the width of the lateral porticoes, and which communicated with a series of rooms whose function must have been related to the square. On the long sides the roofing sloped towards the inside of the square. Rainwater was collected by means of gutters made of blocks of sandstone along the inside of the portico. As far as the use of this square is concerned, we think that it must have been related to the religious healing complex which from the 4$^{th}$ century on had developed around the temple to Asclepius. The urban reforms carried out in the southern sector of the Neapolis towards the middle of the 2$^{nd}$ century BC seem to indicate the wish to give a new impulse to this worship and to incorporate some of the elements that were characteristic of the Hellenistic cities. The similarity between the Emporitan *Asklepieion* and other sanctuaries, such as in the Greek island of Kos, or the Italic city of *Fregellae*, show that the shape of the three successive terraces facilitated the creation of a setting similar to the other healing complexes, in the highest part of which they also built the temple to the protective god – Asclepius. Therefore, this square can be seen as the *abaton*, which is the place where all the sick people who came to be cured assembled.

We have seen that the 2nd century BC was one of the phases in which there was most building activity in Empúries. Apart from the rebuilding of the area of the sanctuaries, there was the construction of a large square, the agora, almost in the centre of the Neapolis. This was a very important development that required the modification of the urban grid of the previous phase. Unfortunately, the information we have on the structure

## Agora and stoa

Aerial view of the central sector of the Neapolis.

and organisation of the city during the centuries that led up to it is very scarce, mainly due to the frequent super-imposition of the remains, meaning that we cannot know precisely whether prior to this there were any areas that could have served the same function as the agora. It is hard to guess the reasons that caused all these changes, but quite clearly the increase in the port activity was one of them, even more so if we bear in mind that the northern limit of this new square was formed by another building of a basically commercial nature – the stoa.

Both constructions are situated at the point where the two main streets of the city meet. Thus, there were three accesses to the square, one in the south that communicated with the street in a south to north direction, and two more at the east and west extremes, that linked with another transversal street. As far as the building of the

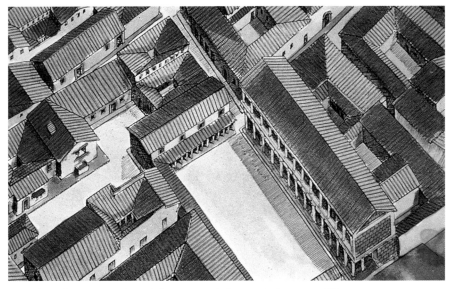

Hypothetical reconstruction of the agora and the stoa (2$^{nd}$ century BC).

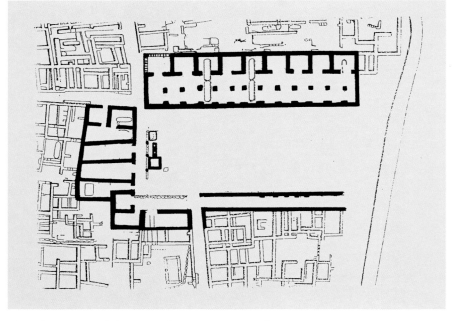

Plan of the agora and the stoa in the Emporitan Neapolis.

Inscription on stone saying ΘΕΜΙΔΟΣ, "of Themis", a reference to the Greek goddess of law. It was probably placed, together with an image of this deity, in an area near the agora, which was used as a court of justice.

agora was concerned, it must have required a great amount of earth to cover up the remains of ancient houses to make up a flat surface. It was a rectangular space, of about 50 by 40 metres, open in the centre and surrounded by a portico that was about four metres wide, of which only the wall that was the foundation for the columns is preserved. The west side, unlike the others, was built from blocks of sandstone and four column bases still survive, about two and a half metres apart, just in front of which are the remains of some bases for statues or altars. There is also a well, the rim of which is beside the front part of the columns of the portico.

Originally agorae were more of a meeting place than a commercial centre, however over time the commercial aspect became very relevant. Therefore, it is not strange that *Emporion*, taking advantage of this moment of economic zenith, should have wanted to include one of the most significant elements of other Hellenistic cities and to reaffirm, at the same time, its origin, at exactly the same time as the Roman culture started to dilute it. In fact, the only notable building is the stoa, which is in the north and which delimits the agora on this side. It is a **14**

Reconstruction of the peristyle house, in the central area of the Neapolis.

building with a rectangular plan, about 50 metres long by 14 metres wide, with nine rooms at the back. that are fairly regular in size. These rooms were used for the traders' meetings and transactions. Below the floor level we can see the remains of the three large cisterns that were built during the same period, which have rectangular bases with rounded corners. The ducts for extracting the water were inside the double gallery of columns which communicated with the square, of which we can only see the foundations, which were made of great blocks of calcareous stone. The size of the bases of the interior columns lead us to believe that there was a second floor. The portico on the façade was supported above a wall which was contemporary to those of the agora and on which we can see the bases for the columns, which coincide with the interior columns; in other words, there were a total of twelve.

## Domestic architecture in the Neapolis

The urban grid that corresponds to the last phase of the Neapolis is fairly well known to us, as its structures were uncovered during the excavations. The domestic architecture reflects to a strong degree the society that characterises this little commercial city in its last phase, which started soon after the arrival of the Romans at Empúries. In fact, the great majority of the buildings, both public and private, that can be visited today are from the

2nd century BC onwards, whilst the effective occupation of the Neapolis does not seem to have gone beyond the first decades of the first century AD. Unfortunately the poor state of preservation of the remains often makes it difficult to interpret the layout of the different dwelling structures.

The simplest kind of domestic dwelling, and also the most numerous, corresponds to the commercial or craftsmen's premises (*tabernae*) which were placed on either side of the city streets and which were probably used as homes too. There were also an important group of houses, on the whole simple ones, with two or more rooms grouped around a small open court. Only in a few of the examples do some of the elements enable us to consider the influence of typological schemes that are well known in the context of 2nd century BC Mediterranean domestic architecture.

Some of these houses were organised around larger courts with porticoes, rather similar to the Hellenistic house with a peristyle. The house to the south of the agora is especially noteworthy, with a central court that was relatively wide and surrounded by columns, which have been partially rebuilt. At the back a large space in an axial position makes up the main reception room, possibly used as a banquet hall.

In another group of houses that are preserved in the Neapolis the presence of a small impluvium in the centre of the flooring of the interior court is significant. This was

Floor with the Greek inscription HΔΥΚΟΙΤΟΣ, meaning "how sweet it is to be reclined", enabling us to interpret this room as a small Greek-style banquet hall for *symposia* (2nd and 1st centuries BC).

used to collect rainwater and to channel it to underground cisterns. Sometimes the impluvium was surrounded by a small portico with four columns. The main room in the house, which was used as a reception room, opened on to one of the laterals of the interior court. These elements lead us to think of the Italic model of the atrium house, adapted for use here in a particular way, given the limitation of available space. Some of these houses were situated on the west side of the Neapolis, where we can make out House H, which has a kind of small Tuscan atrium, without columns around the central impluvium, and also the House the tetrastyle atrium, which, as its name suggests, conserves the remains of a small portico with four columns. In the so-called House of Inscriptions, to the south of the present Museum, the front part of the building was arranged around a court which was also a Tuscan atrium, whilst on the west side the construction is extended with a small peristyle that rests on the remains of the city's western wall.

The kind of construction used in these domestic structures, and in general all the Emporitan buildings, is characterised by the use of walls made of mud on a lower plinth built of stone. There are few of the decorations that without a doubt distinguished the main areas of these houses in the Neapolis. We can only mention the presence of quite a few floors made of mortar and small pieces of crushed pottery (*opus signinum)*, sometimes decorated with black and white tesserae which made up geometrical patterns. At the entrances to some of the rooms, with the same type of flooring, there were often greetings and good omens in Greek, also done with tesserae.

## The Hellenistic breakwater

We have already mentioned that the main raison d'être for Empúries was specifically its port, and also the fact that after the arrival of the Romans there was an increase in the commercial activity. The massive import of Italic products must have meant the constant coming and going of boats, which most probably meant that the old port of the Greek *polis* needed to be restructured. In fact, we only know the location of it, between Sant Martí and

The port jetty. The exterior faces were large blocks of calcareous stone, which were filled in with little stones and mortar.

the Neapolis, in a kind of natural shelter offered by the topography of the coast. On the west it was delimited by a sudden elevation in the natural rock, which formed a kind of cliff, whilst in the south the drop was somewhat less pronounced.

Thanks to the layout of the city walls, we know the southern and western limits of the Greek city. The northern and eastern limits, on the other hand, are much less clear, which is why the relationship between the city and the port is not quite clear. There is very little we can say about the appearance it must have had during the 5th to 3rd centuries BC. However, between the end of the 2nd century and the beginning of the 1st century BC the city decided to remodel or improve its port installations by the construction of a huge breakwater (situated outside the site itinerary), made with a double face of blocks of calcareous stone filled with concrete. Probably the upper part of the rocky reef on which the structure was set was prepared, not just to make the building of it easier, but also to obtain some of the blocks of stone necessary. The use of concrete or *opus caementicium* in Empúries was not documented until after the arrival of the Romans, and is another piece of information that helps date this structure.

**19**

About 80 metres of the breakwater have been preserved. The number of rows preserved depends on the degree of elevation of the land itself, which is lower at the north end, but it varies between nine in the deepest part and six in the highest part. The width of the wall shows a narrowing before the last two rows, as if the builders had wanted to make a platform from where they could build a second vertical part. To reconstruct the appearance of this work is a difficult task due to the fact that , assuming there are more remains, they must be buried under the sea and covered by a thick layer of sand. Therefore we do not know the full length of it, or its exact location. On the other hand, it is more than likely that there were other subsidiary ports situated in nearby areas, such as in the mouths of the Rivers Fluvià and Ter or in the area of Riells-La Clota (L'Escala).

# The last modifications to the public areas of the Neapolis and other buildings of interest

The architectural aspect of the southern sector of the Neapolis was significantly modified between the end of the 2$^{nd}$ century BC and the first quarter of the next century. In fact, at this time a new temple was built, immediately south of the edicule to Asclepius, with similar dimensions and characteristics. Its foundations show, however, that the floor level was raised in such a way that the level in the square was the same as that of the temples. These considerable earth works radically changed the appearance of the upper terrace. This meant that neither the ancient altar in front of the temple to Asclepius nor the double altar-stone one further to the south could be used any longer, and that they had a larger square. This raising of the level meant the construction of a new access stairway from the existing level in relation to the main street into the city. This stairway, which is partially preserved, is made of blocks of sandstone and is just above the one that previously led to this area.

Large cistern built during the last reforms to the *Asklepieion*, divided into four compartments, inside one of which the statue of Asclepius was found in 1909.

3f

In order to date these reforms we need to study the floo-ring that covered the *cella* of the new temple built just next to the temple to Asclepius, made of *opus signinum* and decorated with white tesserae making a motif of rhombuses framed by broken lines. This floor has a reserved space at the end of the *cella* which must have corresponded to the base where the image of the god was placed. The cult significance of the cistern situated at the foot of the edicule to Asclepius, which is now hid-den under the *pronaos* of the new temple, is made clear by the construction of a new curb allowing it to be used later. What is more difficult to find out is which deity they were worshiping, although obviously the connection with

Remains of the great stairway made of blocks of sandstone built for access to the upper terrace of the sanctuary area, where there was the temple to Asclepius, after the raising of the level between the end of the 2$^{nd}$ century and the beginning of the 1$^{st}$ century BC.

the healing activities of the sanctuary leads us to think that maybe it was dedicated to Hygeia, the Greek goddess of health. The construction of this new temple must have occurred at the same time as the re-flooring of the *cella* of the temple to Asclepius with white tessellated mosaic framed in a strip of *opus signinum* decorated with tesserae forming a geometric design.

Despite the fact that now there are no traces of the level of the floor of the square, we know, thanks to information found in ancient excavation records, that it was *opus signinum*. Another important reform was the construction of a large cistern, with a rectangular plan and rounded corners, placed in front of the *pronaos* of the temples. It was made of large blocks of sandstone lined inside with a layer of *opus signinum* in order to make them more waterproof.  It is subdivided into four compartments, which communicate by means of doors covered by arches. Although they are incomplete, we can assume they were higher, especially if we bear in mind that the

Plaque, written in Latin and Greek, three fragments of which have been recovered and on which we see that someone named Noumas paid for the construction of a sanctuary dedicated to Isis and Zeus Serapis. This inscription should be related to the building of a new temple on the lower terrace of the sanctuary area towards the middle of the 1st century BC.

cistern started just under the floor of the square. The far northern part was delimited by a new portico of which there only remains the bases of some columns that possibly were used for lodging the sick people who visited the sanctuary. In the southern part of the square there are also the remains of some buildings, but we cannot be precise about their function.

Soon after the reforms we have just described, around the middle of the 1st century BC, there were major changes to the lower terrace. As we have seen, the configuration of a square surrounded by a portico was possible thanks to moving the walls further south, and now this was to be modified by adding a temple at the far west. Of

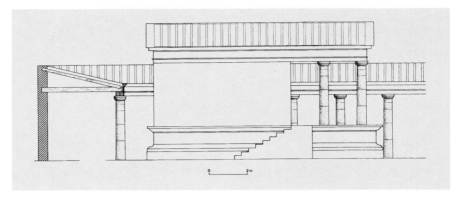

Section of the appearance the lower terrace of the area of the sanctuaries must have had after the construction of the temple to Isis and to Zeus Serapis, towards the middle of the 1$^{st}$ century.

this there still exists a good part of the remains of the podium, at the base of which there is a moulding, and also two access stairs at the side. Its plan allows us to distinguish quite clearly the area for the *cella* and for the *pronaos,* which was made up of four columns at the front portico, complete with two side columns. The addition of the temple to the far east meant the modification of part of the pre-existing portico, with two naves which then became just one, in the same way as the other galleries with porticoes in the square. Regarding the dedication of this new temple, we have found a grey stone tablet, written in Latin and Greek, which mentions that someone called Noumas paid for the building of a temple dedica-

Preserved remains of the temple to Isis and Serapis, with the two side stairways.

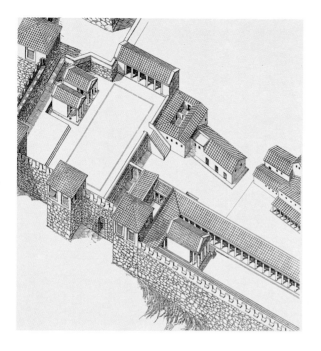

Reconstruction of the southern sector of the Neapolis showing the reforms of the 1st century BC.

ted to Isis and Serapis. It should be mentioned that this inscription was found at the beginning of the excavations, broken into three small pieces which were discovered scattered around the southern sector of the Neapolis. The inscription can be dated back to the middle of the 1st century BC according to epigraphic criteria, and the mention of the construction of or repair to the porticoes leads us to believe that it is directly related to the building of the temple on the lower terrace, which archaeologically speaking we have placed in the same context. Amongst the remains of statues that were recovered in the excavations by Emili Gandia, there were two marble feet that would seem to belong to the seated figure of the god Serapis, accompanied by the dog Cerberus, of which there only remains the left claw. The fact that a sanctuary was dedicated to Serapis should not surprise us given the fact that Noumas was of Alexandrian origin and that there was an association between this worship and that of Asclepius.

## The public cistern

This great cistern was part of a building on the left hand side of the main road that ran from north to south, just before the agora. It was a building which was more or less rectangular and in the middle of which there was a great cistern, with seven rooms organised around it. Two of these rooms, those in the north-east and the south-east corners, give straight onto the main street, while the others were accessed by means of a corridor around the cistern. This cistern, which had a considerable capacity, was made waterproof by adding a layer of *opus signinum,* a paste made from little pieces of crushed pottery mixed with lime, sand and water. It was used for facing the walls and the making the floors of rooms. The cistern collected rainwater from the top of the building, which was most probably covered, as we can tell by the slots for the beams that can be seen at the top. It is possible that there was another floor, which would have been reached by means of a stairway in a small room at the back. This floor would also have communicated with a small street which connected the group of buildings that were furthest to the west, which, due to the particular topography of the Neapolis, were on a higher level. The proximity to the agora, and the fact that some of these rooms can be thought of as having been *tabernae*, lead us to believe that the function of this building was a commercial one.

**12**

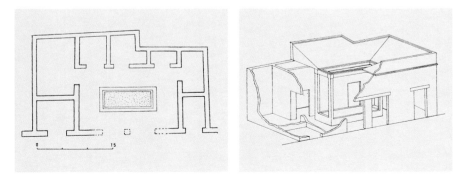

Plan and reconstruction of the public cistern and the market that surrounded it.

Interior of the large public cistern in the Neapolis (2nd and 1st centuries BC).

There was a little fish-salting industry on the main street leading to the agora, on the corner of one of the little streets that went up to the Torre Talaia. Unfortunately, we do not know exactly when it was built, but we do know that it was abandoned in the second half of the 1st century, in the same way as many of the other buildings in the Neapolis. We know that it was a salting factory

## The salting factory

**10**

General view of an industrial building for salting fish, where you can see the small tanks made of bricks and lined with *opus signinum*.

because of the building characteristics and the internal layout of the area. Entrance was from the main street, into an L-shaped warehouse, which surrounded an internal open court. The most interesting remains, which were found in the southern part, are the six side-by-side tanks of differing sizes, made of little stones and covered with *opus signinum*. This type of structure, of which there are many parallel examples in the Mediterranean, was used to salt the fish, which was an essential ingredient in Roman cooking. One of the most appreciated species was tuna fish. The fish was cleaned and chopped up in the interior court and then left in the tanks with the salt and macerated. These conserves could be consumed by the inhabitants of Empúries or exported, for which purpose the fish was stored in amphorae.

### The excavations in the car park

Just in front of the entrance to the Greek city there is a large area, which is currently the car park for visitors to the ruins. Even though it was only sporadically excavated between 1978 and 1984 it offered a great deal of information related to an area which was always outside the city walls. The origin of these excavations lies in the search for answers about the situation of the indigenous settlement, which according to classical sources was just outside the Greek city.

The results obtained provide us with detailed information about the evolution of the sector. In the higher levels

General view of the excavations in the car park area, to the south of the Neapolis.

Small vase containing a treasure made up of 89 silver coins, 88 Roman and one Iberian denarii, found during the excavations in the car park area (end of the 1ˢᵗ century BC).

there was an industrial complex built at the beginning of the 1ˢᵗ century BC, which covered almost the whole of the open rectangle which is visible nowadays. There are still some ovens, pipes and a water well. The remains of the dross found show that this complex was dedicated to lead and silver. Finding this kind of industry outside the fortified site is normal due to the amount of smoke and unpleasant smells it must have produced. The activity was given up towards the middle of the 1ˢᵗ century. The excavation of underlying layers showed the remains of a huge building whose layout and use are not yet known to us, but we can assume that it must have been in use throughout the whole of the 2ⁿᵈ century BC. Underneath this layer, and on the natural rock, a large necropolis was documented, with cremation and burial tombs, dating back to the 4ᵗʰ and 3ʳᵈ centuries BC.

# The Roman city

As we have already mentioned, the end of the Second Punic War meant in practice the beginning of Roman domination in these lands. From this time on Rome would require the indigenous population to pay a series of tributes. The increasing ill-feeling caused by this situation culminated in the revolt of some Iberian tribes in 197 BC which was well and truly crushed by M. Porcius Cato's troops, which landed in the Emporitan port two years later.

Soon after these events a military camp was established on the highest part of Empúries hill. It was set up by the Romans so that they could control the Emporitan port and thus safeguard one of their entrance bases to Hispania. Its construction is directly related to the events that affected this area during the first half of the 2nd century BC. The decision to build a permanent military camp sheltered by the Greek *polis* must be understood as a clear intention to control this territory in a definitive way. On the other hand, the general features of this first establishment were to become, at a later date, the base for the construction of a new city.

The known remains of this camp correspond mainly to the central part, encircled by a wall about two metres wide, built from huge blocks of calcareous stone, of

Cisterns built on large blocks of sandstone, that made up part of the military camp established during the first half of the 2nd century BC.

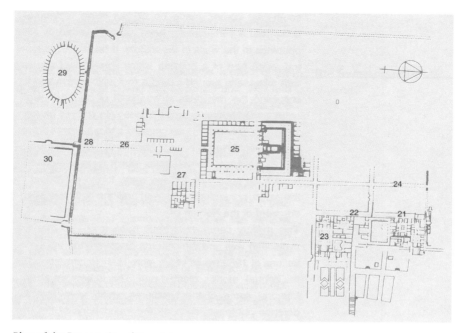

Plan of the Roman city of Empúries.

which in some places you can only see the first row sitting directly on the natural rock. We know about the southeast corner, situated beneath the cryptoportico that surrounded the religious area of the forum of the Roman city, where you can see the corner ashlar that marked the change in direction of the wall towards the west. Archaeology has enabled us the date it to about 175 BC, in other words just a few years after the arrival of the first Italic contingents, and quite a long time before the founding of the Roman city. This is clear because of the way in which it is superimposed on the older structures.

The creation of a new city at the beginning of the 1st century BC led to dismantling a good part of the camp, which is why we cannot establish the exact dimensions and characteristics, as only the part used as the foundations of these new constructions is preserved. We only know a little about the inside of this fortified site, corresponding to a great cistern that was for public use right at the

century, it is also documented as having tombs corresponding to the Late Roman period.

The new situation which came about as a result of the Roman intervention during the Second Punic War and the later Roman dominance over the Mediterranean side of the Iberian peninsula, led to important consequences for *Emporion* and the immediate territory. The ancient Greek colony, although maintaining a certain degree of political independence, was reaffirmed once again in its role of an articulating nucleus in the extreme northeast of the peninsula. Rome took advantage of this fact to take political, military and economic control of the territory itself and to ensure that the commercial routes between the Italian and Iberian peninsulas were kept open. The Emporitan port had a key position on these routes.

Over time, these circumstances would create a new reality which was to crystallise at the turn of the 2nd and 1st centuries BC, from which time we can start to talk about the "Romanisation" of the area. In this context, the crea-

## The founding of the new city

Aerial view of the Roman city.

tion of a new city took place, next to the old Greek settlement. It was shaped in accordance with the lines that up to that time had characterised the urban settlements in the Italian peninsula. This event made clear the desire to maintain the privileged role of the city in the process of its integration into the schemes imposed by Rome for restructuring the provincial territories. However, despite the fact that the urban characteristics of the new city began to be well known, we still do not have enough information on some of the aspects such as the legal-political condition, how the population was made up, the degree of participation of the Italic immigrants, the role that the indigenous element played, or how they adapted to the new reality.

The unquestionable fact is that from this time on Empúries was to become a true "dual city", in which the old *Emporion* (which we should remember included the *Palaiapolis* and the Neapolis) survived as an active port area, due to the high level of Italic commerce still active in the western Mediterranean. This fact justified the improvement to the Emporitan port, and the use of other areas along the coast, such as Riells (to the south of the old part of L'Escala), which were suitable for anchoring commercial vessels. The intensity of this commerce is shown, although only partially, by the materials dug up in excavations, in which the percentage of the imported products (wine amphorae, pottery from Italy, etc.) was fairly high, compared to the local products which, on the other hand, had a relatively extensive area of distribution in the territory itself.

The prosperity that Empúries still enjoyed was also shown in the new public, religious or domestic constructions, that completed the remodelling of the Neapolis during the 2$^{nd}$ and 1$^{st}$ centuries BC. From this time onwards, however, the newly created Roman city would be the representative frame for the new reality of Empúries, following, both in the large dimensions of the public centre and in the private constructions, models that were well established and which tell us a lot about the character of the new settlement.

As a continuation of their policy of urbanisation that originated from Empúries itself, the Romans promoted the creation of other urban establishments throughout the first decades of the 1ˢᵗ century, such as *Gerunda* (Girona), and further to the south *Iluro* (Mataró) or *Baetulo* (Badalona), which were to become backbones of their immediate territory and focuses of culture for the Iberian people. In a parallel way, with the slow but sure disappearance of the indigenous structures, the rural population was shaped according to the Italic *villae* system. These were agricultural settlements that were basically self-sufficient, dedicated to exploiting a specific part of the territory, and at the same time home to the owners and to the farm labourers who worked on the land.

The new city, created at the beginning of the 1ˢᵗ century BC on the large hill that dominated the ancient Greek settlement of Empúries from the west, covered a surface of approximately 22.5 hectares, the limits of which we know perfectly well thanks to the remains of the wall that surrounded the urban nucleus. The building characteristics of this site would seem to exclude a merely military and defensive use, but would rather seem to delimit the *pomerium,* an area consecrated during the founding rituals prior to the creation of a new urban establishment, which had strong religious and juridical connotations.

The best-preserved sector of these walls corresponds to the area that closed off the city to the south, where you can see a plinth made of large polygonal blocks of calcareous stone, possibly taken from the pre-existing quarries around the Emporitan site itself. Above this there was a second level of concrete mixed with small stones, at the base of which you can still see the holes for slotting in the wooden cross bars to support the plank moulding. This upper part of the wall was filled with earth and stones. In more modern times it was hollowed out in some places to be used as a refuge and for building small vine-growers' huts.

In this southern part of the wall there are still the two gates that led into the city. One of them, in the south-east

## The walls of the Roman city

**28**

Entrance to the Roman city. You can still see the tracks left by the wheels of the carts.

corner, is unusual due to being placed obliquely to the grid of the city streets, and possibly this must be explained in relationship to the route of the path which from the west, communicated the city with the territory itself. The other access is at the far south of the main street or *cardo Maximus*, which led straight to the public centre or city forum. In this entrance, of a reduced width, which was originally protected by an internal bastion, you can still see the wheel marks made by the carriages going through it. To the right of the entrance you can also see, sculpted in relief, a phallic representation, that is repeated a few metres further west. These were protective symbols, also found in other Italic defensive sites, which were supposed to invoke the protection and prosperity of the city.

The western and northern parts of the wall are less known, even though the remains of the plinth and the blocks of *opus caementicium* allow us to follow its course. The closure in the eastern part was partially dismantled due to the linking up of the two nuclei, the Greek and the Roman ones, that became one single site, which happened, as we will see later, a few decades after the founding of the Roman city. The partial dismantling of this section allowed them to extend the urbanised area to the east, as can be seen by the fact that some extensions of the large houses dug up in the Roman city are superimposed on the foundations of the ancient wall.

Further to the north of the so-called "House number 1", there are other remains of the city wall which, from a constructive point of view, have different characteristics from the rest of the perimeter around the city. Here the height of the stone plinths in some places is higher than three metres. In fact, the northern sector of the Roman city appears, at least in the initial phase, to be separated from the rest by means of an inner wall, which runs transversely to the others mentioned, which was also based on a plinth of blocks of calcareous stone. Some of the remains of this transversal wall are visible in the plot of land to the east of Roman house number 1, just where *cardo B* starts. What were the reasons for this internal wall? One hypothesis is that the northern sector was the area that was set aside for the indigenous population who had integrated in the city, although they were still a separate group. The final solution to this and other historical questions will however, have to wait for future excavations.

Detail of the face of the wall and the phallus sculpted onto one of the blocks to the right of the entrance to the Roman city.

## The streets

The founding of the city meant, apart from the physical boundaries of the urban area, the planning of the streets. The large area of land the city occupied was divided into sections by a network of orthogonal streets, in islands of a rectangular shape ready for future buildings *(areae or insulae)*. This regular urban grid is well documented thanks to the excavations in some areas of the city, which have confirmed the systematic planning at the same time as the city was being created. The islands or *insulae*, accurately designed north-to-south, were bounded by six wide parallel streets crossing the city longitudinally *(cardines)*, and the other series of east-to-west streets *(decumani)* at right-angles to them. The orientation of these streets seems to have been largely determined by pre-existing structures, which as we have men-

**24**

Aerial view of the excavations of the so-called *cardo B* of the Roman city, one of the main axes that went through the city from north to south

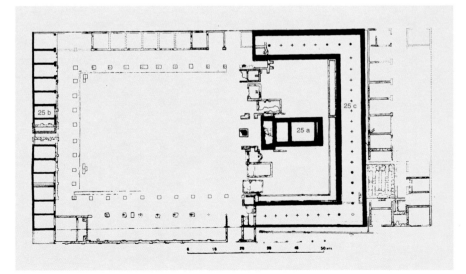

Plan of the forum area in the Late Republican period.

tioned before, have been interpreted as the remains of an ancient military camp that dates back to the 2nd century BC.

The size of the *insulae*, approximately 70 metres long and 35 metres wide, show the use of Roman metrology (2 per 1 *actus:* an *actus* is equivalent to 120 Roman feet, in other words 35.48 metres, each Roman foot being 29.6 cm). The urban plan made provision, from the very beginning, for places for the city's public areas, especially the forum, framework of the main public and religious buildings that took up an area corresponding to four of the central *insulae* in the southern sector. The access to this great public square was by the main street or *cardo Maximus,* which began at the gate in the centre of the south wall. Along the length of this street, and also in other of the city's arteries, there were a large number of premises dedicated to various craft and commercial activities (*tabernae*), which opened directly onto the streets or were sometimes separated by a modest portico, which tells us about the daily activity of the city, in contrast to other residential sectors.

The development and composition of the public centre of the Roman city, which we will explain here, is based mainly on the results of the excavations in this sector in 1982 and 1983. Despite this, the most recent work carried out in this square, with the purpose of unearthing

**26**

## The Forum area: the Late Republican period

Iberian pottery container painted with concentric semicircles. This form, known as *kalathos,* was one of the most characteristic of this type (2nd and 1st centuries BC).

Terracotta antefix in Hellenistic style found inside one of the silos, re-filled when the Roman city was created. It must have been part of the architectural decoration of a previous building (2nd century BC).

**25b**

Reconstruction of the northern sector of the Republican forum, with the Capitoline temple, the portico and the cryptoportico, which formed the area of worship.

most of the buildings that made it up, shows that the sequence is considerably more complex than could have been imagined until not long ago, mainly as far as the oldest phases are concerned. The current state of archaeological research, that is still ongoing, warns us to be prudent and to keep the first global interpretation, at least until any new conclusions can be reached.

The definition of this public area is based, from the first moment of the founding of the Roman city, on the existence of an uncovered area, corresponding to the two *insulae* and very probably serving as a framework for the main public affairs. The east and west boundaries of this first square are not at all well known due to the reforms in later periods, and also to the lack of correlation with the original constructions. In the south, on the other hand, we are sure about the existence of a series of premises of a uniform size, laid out in an ordered style which we suppose were for commercial use.

In the north of the square a religious area was reserved, in the centre of which there was a great temple, exactly axial to the main street and possibly dedicated to the official worship of the Capitoline Triad – Jupiter, Juno and Minerva. This temple which architecturally was typically

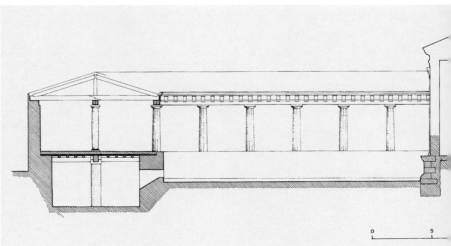

Aerial view of the forum. In the foreground the U-shaped building corresponds to the cryptoportico.

Italic, was built on a raised podium and lined on the outside with a parament of ashlars of sandstone. At present there are only the remains of the internal stones and mortar filler, as well as some ashlars corresponding to

**25a**

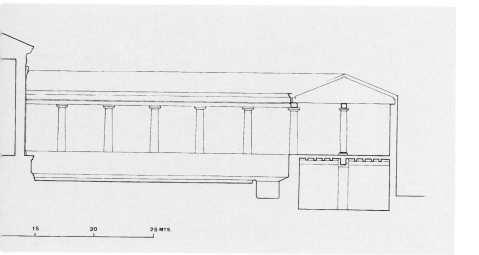

15   20   25 MTS.

the base of the exterior face, delimited by a *cyma reversa* moulding. This was a temple of a tetrastyle kind (with a front portico of four columns), prostyle (with columns only around the vestibule or *pronaos),* and pseudoperipter (with pilasters joined to the outer part of the *cella).* The columns and pilasters seem to have been of the Corinthian order, according to the definitive configuration of the temple that took place in a later reform, dating to the third quarter of the 1st century BC. It is interesting to point out the use of a metrology of a central Italic origin –with the unit of measurement corresponding to an oscan foot of 27.5 cm- by the builders of this great religious structure that dominated the city's first forum.

The images of the gods were placed on a little base located in the background of *cella.* In front of the *pronaos* the podium formed a wider platform, with access in the centre, in front of which there was an altar. The pre-eminent

**25c**

position of the temple in relation to the architectural layout of the forum was completed by a portico which delimited the sacred area or *temenos,* and consisted of a double row of columns which was supported over a lower gallery or cryptoportico. Daylight and air from outside entered this semi-underground corridor thanks to the trapezoid shaped skylights that opened into the intercolumns of the upper portico. Of these cryptoporticoes

View of Roman house number 1. In the foreground you can see the lower sector of the house.

there are only the remains situated at a lower level and the central row of columns made of cylindrical tambours above which the beams that supported the flooring of the upper gallery were placed.

The urban planning of the new city also determined the occupation of the *insulae* by the first private buildings. Of all the islands occupied by dwellings, we currently only know about two that were on the east side of the city. These correspond to houses number 1, 2A and 2B. The oldest parts show us that the configuration of the first houses in the city followed the traditional model of Italic houses with a central atrium. The existence of these houses is explained by the important role played in the new settlement by the social group that was directly affected by the increase in the commercial activity in the Emporitan port. These local privileged elite, made up of a group of Italic origin, tried to reflect in their houses the styles that, both architecturally and decoratively, characterised private houses in those times in the central area of the Italian peninsula. On the other hand, the layout of the houses, with the main entrances open to the eas-

### The first houses in the Roman city

The Late Republican atrium of Roman house number 1. In the foreground you can see one of the rims of the impluvium cisterns.

Tuscan atrium of Roman house number 2B, in which the cover was not supported by columns.

 ternmost *cardo* of the city, and placed in a west-east posi-tion, in other words, transversal to the longitudinal axis of the *insulae,* seemed to reflect the original division of the plots of land destined to be occupied by domestic buil-dings.

The oldest nucleus of house number 1 is characterised by being built on two terraces, thereby overcoming the difference in levels. The upper terrace was occupied by the sector that represented the *domus*, distributed around the interior court or atrium, partially uncovered, that allowed the rooms around it to be aired and receive daylight. The opening in the covering, the compluvium, was directly over a shallow, rectangular tank, the implu-vium, in the centre, where they collected rainwater and from which the water was channelled to the two cisterns below the floor of the atrium. All around the portico around the impluvium there was a little portico of four co-lumns, one at each corner of the main tank. During a later reform the impluvium was increased to six columns. The rooms of the atrium area were arranged in a per-fectly regular and symmetric way. The entrance corridor (*fauces*) was just in front of the room known as the tabli-num, the main reception and representative area of the house, another of the essential elements in an Italic atrium house.

The rooms in this "noble" area of the *domus* were deco-rated with painted murals, although there are very few

Detail of the floor of one of the rooms in Roman house number 1, made of *opus signinum,* and decorated with black and white tessellations. At the back, the area reserved for the bed.

remains. There are still some of the floors, made of mortar and small fragments of pottery *(opus signinum)* and sometimes decorated with geometric motifs made with small black and white tesserae. On either side of the tablinum there were two small rooms, in which the floor decoration was done in such a way as to leave an area at the end of the room, possible for a bed, thus their function was as bedrooms or *cubicula.*

The lower terrace, for domestic use and service, was accessible by means of a narrow corridor parallel to the retention wall in the higher area, corresponding to the atrium sector. However, originally there was independent

Polychromatic mosaics showing a theatrical mask and a partridge taking jewels out of a basket. These small mosaic pictures of Hellenistic inspiration decorated the floors of some rooms in house number 1 (1$^{st}$ century BC).

access from the outside to this part of the house, which was walled up in a later reform. During the first phase of occupation of the island containing the house number 1 we must imagine the existence of other similar domestic

Polychromatic mosaic showing the mythological scene of the sacrifice of Iphigenia at Aulis. It comes from a house in the Roman city, which has still not been excavated, and must have decorated the floor in one of the main rooms (1$^{st}$ century BC).

buildings that occupied neighbouring plots and of which there are hardly any remains, due to the extension works carried out later by the owners of this great *domus*.

The original division of the land is possibly more evident in the island situated further south, here we can see, in line with each other, two atrium houses, corresponding to the oldest parts of houses 2A and 2B. To these we should add a third *domus*, which almost completely disappeared during the last extension to the Roman house number 1.

**22-23**

There are still some remains of Roman house number 2A, arranged around a great central atrium that could be attributed to the Late Republican period, even though their general appearance is the result of later reforms that were to cover up the original layout. In fact, a large part of this plot was occupied by the extension of the *domus* situated to the south, known as house number 2B. The atrium of this dwelling, dating to the beginning of the 1$^{st}$ century BC, reflects even more clearly the application of the traditional scheme of the Italic atrium *domus,* with all its characteristic elements. In this case it is a Tuscan atrium, without columns, around a small central impluvium with a coloured mosaic floor, in which there were irregular fragments of different coloured marble. The atrium, which was square, was extended on either side with two *alae,* areas that opened straight onto the central court, which were another of the traditional elements of Italic style houses. The layout of the rooms follows a very regular pattern, especially on either side of the tablinum, where they repeated the association of a room designed for banquets or triclinium, with a reception room or exedra which was square. The importance of these "noble" areas in the house was also emphasised by the painted decorations that adorned the walls, of which there are still a few panels that can be classified in the so-called 2$^{nd}$ Pompeian style. The floors, also made of *opus signinum,* sometimes had a tessellated decoration with a geometric motif. These rooms, together with the tablinum, must have originally opened onto a porticoed corridor that may have led to a garden or *hortus* that occupied the back part of the plot.

**23**

# The *municipium Emporiae*

In the middle of the 1st century BC an important event was to mark the beginning of a new stage in the development of the city. According to the Roman historian Titus Livius, there was the establishment of a contingent of veteran soldiers licensed from Julius Caesar's army that up to now had been fighting in the Iberian peninsula against the rebel troops led by the sons of Pompey, who they finally defeated in the Battle of Munda in 45BC. This event, almost certainly motivated by Caesar's desire to ensure control over the area and of faithfulness to the city so as to neutralise any possible opposition during the conflict, was the origin of a series of fundamental changes which in a short time crystallised into a new juridical-political reality – the *municipium Emporiae*. Under this new situation the city became integrated into the new policy of the reorganisation of the provincial territory which happened to a great extent during Augustus' reign. Archaeology also reflects these events. There is documentation about various inscriptions that refer to esta-

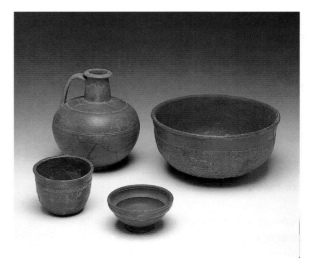

Pottery vases known as *Terra Sigillata*, table crockery that was typical of the Roman Imperial period, from different areas of production in Italy, the south of France and the north of Africa (towards the end of the 1st century BC – 2nd century AD).

Bronze plaque dedicated to *Lucius Minicius Rufus,* mentioning the various municipal posts he held: *aedil* (in charge of watching over public areas and markets), *duovir* ( a post equivalent to that of present day mayors), *quaestor* (in charge of financial matters and administering the public treasury) and *flamen* (priest) of public worship to Rome and Augustus (1ˢᵗ century).

blishing patronages with important people from the provincial administration, directly linked to the most influential political circles at that time, and later with the Imperial family. Numismatics also offers unquestionable evidence of the transformation of the city into a Roman municipality as the coins bore the inscription *MUNICI EMPORIA*. The different sectors of the Emporitan town became integrated in this new juridical framework, as Roman citizens with full rights. Following the words of Titus Livius "now they are confused in just one body, having been accepted as Roman citizens, first the native Hispanics and then, later, the Greeks".

From a topographical point of view, these events reflect the unification of the two nuclei that up to then had been separate – the old Greek settlement, which would now lose its relative independence as a federated city, and the Roman city, which had been created a few decades previously. This unification meant that the walls that separated the two cities became redundant, and that a new common wall was built, which is in a very poor state

Marble statue of a municipal "magistrate" of the Roman city of Empúries, found in the forum area. He is wearing a toga and on his right there is a cylindrical box of *volumina*, where the documents relating to town matters were kept (1ˢᵗ century).

of preservation, which goes from the corner of the southern wall of the Neapolis along to the limit of the Roman city, thereby forming a single site. The plural of the city name *Emporiae* (the Empúries), which is found in written documents, is significant of this evolution.

In this context we must situate the important reforms that affected both the public and the private areas. The forum was remodelled almost definitively, showing the desire of the city to adapt to the policy of monumentalisation affecting the main provincial towns during the first Imperial period. However, the circumstances that had favoured the development as an urban nucleus up until then were now starting to lose importance, slowly but surely, in particular the privileged role of the Emporitan port in relation to Italic commerce in this sector of the Western Mediterranean. The changes in the flow of commerce, with an ever increasing important part played by products made in provincial territories, together with the consolidation of other centres as focal points for the new structuring of the area, were to mean the beginning of the process of decline for Empúries and the decreasing importance that became more and more evident.

Throughout the first century, the construction of some public buildings, most probably paid for by members of the elite citizens who occupied the main municipal magistracies, could be considered as an indication of some kind of dynamism. This is the case of the modest amphitheatre and the palaestra that are to be found in the southern limit of the city in the Julius-Claudius period, and the new small temples raised in the forum during the Flavian period. The construction characteristics of these buildings show, however, the limited resources that the city was facing, from this time on.

The last quarter of the first century was to mark an important increase in the process of decline of the city, and the obligation to adapt itself to a completely different situation. The consequences of the urban crisis became increasingly evident, and one example of this is the collapse of some of the forum buildings and the definitive abandonment of a large part of the city, beginning with the Neapolis itself which, it would seem, was not inhabited after the Flavian period. Throughout the 2nd century, the depopulation of the Roman city also extended to the sector occupied by the large houses owned by the local oligarchy, who were now unable to keep them up. Despite all this, certain areas of the city, especially the streets nearest the centre, were still frequented until the third quarter of the 3rd century, although they now had a very different character, which cannot be described as a truly urban life. The limited nature of this late occupation of the city has to be ascribed to its subsidiary function with regard to other residential areas that were now established in other parts of the Emporitan topography and that would continue throughout the Late Roman and Mediaeval periods, mainly in Sant Martí d'Empúries.

The changes observed in the public centre of the city were a reflection of its historic evolution during the last decades of the Late Republican period and the beginning of the Imperial period. The first important modification that altered the layout of the old square especially concerned the most emblematic building, the Capitoline temple. This is the reform that was made in the third quarter of the 1st century BC, in the area of worship which previously opened onto the square and which was now separated by the construction of a wall, in which there was a gap only in front of the temple. Access to the interior of the religious area was, therefore, restricted and was by means of two small entrances situated on either side of the altar. These changes also led to modifications in the access to the temple, by the construction of two side stairways allowing access to the front of the podium from the back. This reform, which probably affected the exterior aspect of the temple, must be related to the consequences that the installation of Caesarean settlers meant. The new aspect of the temple has led us to believe that there was a fundamental change in the dedication of the building, which from now on would have been dedicated to the worship of Caesar deified.

## The Augustan Forum

25d

Fragment of what might have been the Emporitan municipal law, from the Augustan period, that mentions how the patrons of the city are to be elected. It was written on a sheet of bronze, and would have been on public display in the forum of the city.

The most important reform done to the forum, an example of the consolidation of the new municipality, must be dated to the Augustan period, in the last quarter of the 1$^{st}$ century BC. The central open area, paved with slabs of sandstone, was surrounded by an porticoed *ambulacrum* in Ionic style. As a result, the architectural reconstruction that we can see today in this sector is not fully consistent with the archaeological interpretation of it. The row of *tabernae* that during the previous phase communicated directly with the interior of the forum were still in use, although access was now from the street, so that the commercial function was transferred to outside the public centre. The forum became an area that was susceptible to being on the sidelines of the city's daily activities, through doors that were placed at its three main entrances, and the focus was placed on the role of a representative framework for the political, administrative and religious life. In this way, the inclusion of a new building, the basilica, used for the administration of justice and other municipal matters, was significant. This basilica was discovered in one of the laterals of the forum, separated from the wing that faced the portico by means of a second row of columns, of which just the foundations

25f

remain, together with the remains of some bases for statues. The basilica was, in fact, made of one long nave, with a separate room at the southern extreme, which was accessible through a small vestibule. This area was used as a justice tribunal, symbolically presided over by the image of the emperor (*aedes Augusti),* and was possibly also used as a meeting place for members of the municipal council (*decuriones).*

The Augustan reform of the Emporitan forum also shows the importance of Imperial worship as a determining element in the new architectural and monumental concept of the public centre of the city. Thus, right alongside the old Republican temple, there were two small temples which completed the religious area. One of them was possibly dedicated to the official worship of Rome and Augustus, as shown in the double compartmenting of the *cella.*

The important remodelling of the forum, which took place in the first decades of the Imperial period, also affected

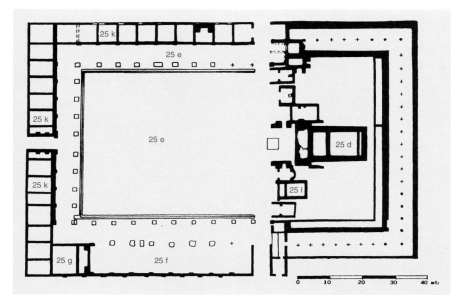

Plan of the forum in Augustan times.

the nearer areas, where there were different areas laid out in order to channel commercial activity and the handicrafts outside the public centre. Rows of premises or *tabernae* opened directly on to the streets around the forum, which without doubt were the most frequented streets of the city. In the north, a double row of premises on either side of a narrow street seems to have been a small market or *macellum,* situated next to the public cisterns of the Republican period.

Throughout the 1st century, the new buildings that were built in the forum did not significantly alter the appearance that has just been described. Little temples of a modest nature were built, which definitively closed off the northern limit of the public square. We only know the dedication of one of them, thanks to an inscription that tells us of the existence of the worship of the goddess Tutela. Some of these temples are founded on the ruins of the cryptoportico, half buried in Flavian times, and thus masking the signs of a clear crisis. This process of progressive degradation of the monumental centre of the city continued during the 2nd century and affected the rest of the buildings of the forum, such as the portico that limited the square that was built during the Augustan reform. Without doubt, this is conclusive evidence of the lack of resources from which the city suffered, due to which it was now unable to undertake the necessary reconstruction of its public buildings.

## The great *domus* of the Imperial period

The historical evolution of Empúries during the first Imperial period is also reflected in the changes affecting the domestic architecture of the Roman city. However, we must admit that the knowledge we have is partial due to the small number of houses that have been excavated to date. On the other hand, the image they present almost always corresponds to that of the great houses belonging to the local oligarchy. In fact, some of the old atrium houses, which are characteristic of the initial phase of the city, soon started the extending process encroaching on the space occupied by other houses, and even went beyond the limits of the *insulae*. Thanks

Black and white mosaic floors with geometric motifs, from the northern part of Roman house number 1.

to these successive extensions the richest houses in the Roman city had new suites of rooms and reception areas, often grouped around gardened and porticoed areas. The architectural solutions used, together with the decorating techniques for the floor and murals, show how the dominant fashions in domestic architecture were followed by the Emporitan urban elite, who wanted to show off their privileged position through their houses.

The first main reforms to the houses on the eastern side of the Roman city consisted of the inclusion of spacious open areas surrounded by porticoes or peristyles, an element inspired by Hellenistic models, which had become one of the essential components in the model of the Italic aristocratic houses during the last Late Republican period. The old atriums, which preserved the original layout to a great degree, kept their traditional role as a reception area, and were, at the same time, an elegant vestibule to access the interior of the house.

The great peristyle of Roman house number 1 has the peculiarity that it is based on a lower cryptoportico, which  also had four wings. This solution allowed the sector to

Aerial view of Roman hou-
ses numbers 2A and 2B.

be levelled, therefore overcoming the difference in the levels. The central garden, of a considerable size, was surrounded by wide porticoes, whilst the northern side opened onto a set of "noble" rooms for entertaining the urban elite, such as the *triclinia* banquets. The decoration of these rooms is a good example of the degree of refinement of Emporitan mansions during the first decades of the city life. There are remains of the paintings that were on the walls, which fitted in with the second Pompeian style. As well as floors using *signinum* deco-

Aerial view of Roman house
number 1. In the centre
foreground you can see the
great peristyle.

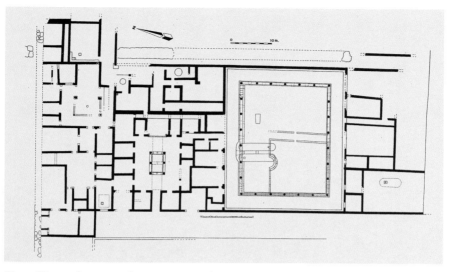

Plan of Roman house number 1, corresponding to its later phase (1ˢᵗ and 2ⁿᵈ centuries).

rated with geometric motifs, we can find mosaics entirely tessellated with a white background, decorated with simple black borders and with coloured square mosaics made out of tiny tessellations (*opus vermiculatum*), reproducing well-known Hellenistic-inspired motifs.

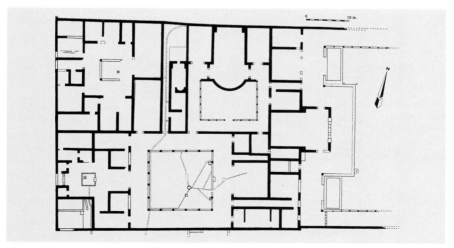

Plans of Roman houses number 2A and 2B (1ˢᵗ and 2ⁿᵈ centuries).

One of the pillars (a ḥerm) sculpted in the shape of a female body, on which portraits were put. They come from Roman house number 2B, where they lined the entrance to one of the main reception rooms, symmetrically (1ˢᵗ century).

In later developments to Roman house number 1, new sets of rooms were added, grouped around the different nuclei of distribution. In the northern sector of the house, built in the first century, are the remains of an important set of black and white mosaics which develop different geometric motifs, next to some samples which are not as well preserved, of flooring made with small slabs of stone *(opus sectile)*. Finally, at the end of the 1ˢᵗ century a new set of rooms was built in the southern area of the peristyle, thus completing the definitive form of the house. The modest construction characteristics of this part of the house would seem to suggest a certain limitation in the resources. However, there are also some rooms which still preserve mosaic floors with geometric decoration and we should point out the presence, in an axial position, of an enormous area possibly used for summer banquets, due to the fact that it is facing north.

House 2B follows a similar kind of development. Here also, the house was originally laid out around an atrium and was extended with new rooms opening onto different peristyles, which occupied the whole of the available area of the island and took up part of the neighbouring plot of land, extending beyond the original limit that showed the situation of the perimeter city wall. In fact, the construction of the first peristyle, laid out along the same longitudinal axis as the atrium, meant the destruction of that part of the wall, a phenomenon which must have been related to the unification of the two Emporitan nuclei in the second half of the 1ˢᵗ century BC. A second smaller peristyle was built later on the northern side, communicating with a group of three large rooms symmetrically laid out. We should note the presence of a small thermal complex *(balneum)* belonging to the house, made up of three rooms. The northern one was used for hot baths *(caldarium)*, as can be deduced from the layout and the presence of a hot air chamber or hypocaust under the floor. Finally, the third peristyle seems to surround a large garden *(hortus)* which extends to the east and which definitively classified this house as a true suburban villa.

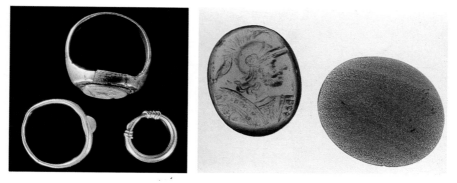

Roman jewels made of silver and gold, and stones for rings engraved with tiny figures or mythological scenes.

The growth of the area of these *domus* is, therefore, the result of several different phases of construction from the second half of the 1$^{st}$ century BC to the beginning of the 2$^{nd}$ century. From this time, however, the progressive crises that affected the city, and which was to intensify throughout this century, were to cause a rapid abandonment of those luxurious mansions, which was to become one of the most eloquent manifestations of the new situation to which Empúries had to adapt.

The structures excavated on one of the islands situated to the south-east of the forum, of a very different nature to the great houses we have mentioned, present an

**27**

A private portrait of a female in bronze, found in the Roman city of Empúries. The type of hairstyle, with lots of curls framing the face and the rest of the hair plaited and pulled back into a bun, allows us to date it to the last third of the 1$^{st}$ century. The original is in the Museu d'Arqueologia de Catalunya-Barcelona.

image that although limited, helps us understand the different characteristics of the domestic units that belonged to the less privileged sectors of the social make-up of the city. Here we can see, next to the usual line up of premises or *tabernae,* houses of a more modest nature, both with regard to the area and to the architectural layout, although there are some rooms that are noteworthy, with decorated floors and paintings.

Domestic altar, decorated with paintings, from the garden of the peristyle of Roman house number 2B. On one of its sides there is a cock, whilst on the opposite side there is a small vase with a long stem and handles (a crater) which contains a pineapple surrounded by snakes, whose bodies continue round to the other two sides.

Towards the middle of the 1ˢᵗ century two new public buildings were constructed outside the Roman city. They
were situated next to the southern face of the wall, on
both sides of the main entrance. They were a modest
amphitheatre for gladiatorial fights and a palaestra, an
area for doing gymnastic exercises. The characteristics
of these buildings, which were not all that large, show us
quite clearly that there was a lack of resources in the
municipality to pay for them. Despite this, by building
these constructions, the city tried to have the architectural elements of prestige that were characteristic of provincial cities, as well as to meet the demands of the growing popularity of gladiatoral games.

The remains of the amphitheatre consist of a series of
walls radiating out from the wall that marked out the central oval surface that was the arena. The function of
these radial walls was to support the seats, that we assume were made of wood. The main entrances to the
arena, through which the gladiators must have paraded,
were situated at either end of the longitudinal axis of the
building, whilst there was a third door, of a secondary
nature, that opened to the north side, facing the lesser
axis of the arena.

The narrowness of the grades was compensated for by
the large area, which meant the arena was of exceptio-
nal size, with a maximum of 74 metres from east to west
and 44.4 metres from north to south (250 x 150 Roman
feet). However, the capacity of the Emporitan amphithe-

### The amphitheatre and the palaestra

**29**

A bronze anthropomorphic
lamp, with silver appliqués
for the eyes and earrings. In
the upper part there is a
large rosette that surrounded the opening into which
the oil that fed the wick was
poured (1ˢᵗ century).

Structures that made up the base of the amphitheatre of Empúries (mid 1st century).

atre, estimated at little more than 3,300 spectators, was very limited in comparison to the great amphitheatres in the main Hispanic cities, which were much larger.

As far as the palaestra is concerned, the building consisted of a large uncovered rectangular area, 100 metres long by 55 metres wide, which was used for practising physical exercises such as races, gymnastics, fights and so on. Around it there was a gallery, which may have had porticoes, although there are very few remains.

Remains of the walls of the palaestra or gymnasium (middle of the 1st century).

Once the Roman city had been created at the beginning of the 1$^{st}$ century BC new areas of necropolises formed outside the urban area, alongside the paths that led away from the city gates (outside the site that you are visiting). Unfortunately, a great number of these tombs were plundered by clandestine excavators during the 19$^{th}$ century and the beginning of the 20$^{th}$ century. Despite this, some parts of these cemeteries have been excavated, and in order to distinguish the different areas, they were given the names of the owners of the land on which the tombs were found (Rubert, Ballesta, Torres, Nofre necropolises and so on). However, in fact they are all part of the same area that extended along the western and southern slopes of the hill occupied by the Roman city.

The funeral rite that characterised these necropolises in the first centuries of the life of the city was almost exclusively cremation. The ashes of the deceased were placed in an urn, almost always made of pottery, covered with a lid, either a plate of just a stone. However, there are also some glass urns, protected inside lead boxes. The cinerary urns were buried along with other objects that made up the funeral goods, which were generally rather poor. There were usually small recipients for ointment, made of glass or pottery, a few coins and personal belongings such as rings, earrings, pendants and so on. The type of tombs were also fairly simple. The urns were laid out, wedged in place with stones, inside the graves dug into the earth. Only in a few cases was the grave marked on the outside by a small cubic base, sometimes topped off with a hemisphere. Inside these simple funeral monuments, built and painted red on the outside, one or several cinerary urns were placed.

Despite the fact that the majority of the burials in the necropolises of the Roman city were cremations, there were also some inhumation tombs, with the body of the deceased laid out in a simple grave or protected by sloping tiles along each side. There has also been documentation of burials inside re-used amphorae, generally in the case of children. These tombs did not often con-

## The necropolises situated around the Roman city

Roman lamps from the 1st century.

Glass containers from the Roman period found in the excavations at Empúries (1st and 2nd centuries).

A pottery cinerary urn and ointment vases from the Ballesta necropolis, one of the burial areas from High Imperial times, to the west of the Roman city.

tain funeral goods which makes it difficult to date them. Although some of the burials seem to be from the 2nd century, these rites generally took place in the Late Roman period, which is when the Roman city had been abandoned.

## Late Roman and Mediaeval Empúries

After the long process of abandoning the urban areas during the High Imperial period, the Late Roman city of Empúries became reduced to what is today the nucleus of Sant Martí d'Empúries. In fact, this is the only sector in the Emporitan site that has been continuously occupied up to the present day. Throughout the enormous extensions to the Roman city, built at the beginning of the 1st century BC we have found no indication that it was inhabited after the third quarter of the 3rd century. In the Neapolis however, after a long process of abandonment and natural covering of the ancient urban structures by the "sands of time", there was from the 4th century onwards the introduction of a large cemetery and the construction of a small building for Christian worship.

### The Late Roman cemetery and the *cella memoriae* of the Neapolis

One of the funeral chambers next to the *cella memoriae,* where you can see the stone sarcophaguses with the double-sided sloped lids, decorated with simple acroteria.

The cemetery where the inhabitants of the city of Empúries were buried until the Muslim occupation, was concentrated in the northern sector of the ancient Neapolis and it extends towards the west. Of the more than five hundred tombs recorded, with a variety of burial methods (in amphorae, in boxes made of stone slabs, in *tegulae,* in simple graves, in wooden boxes, or in sarcophaguses of various kinds), nowadays only the stone sarcophaguses in the funeral chambers placed around the little cemetery church are visible. Most of the burials, particularly those that were on top of the architectural remains of the Neapolis, were excavated in the period prior to 1936 and were not preserved *in situ.*

However, the documentation from that era has enabled us to study the characteristics of the cemetery and we should point out the careful planning of the burials and the almost complete lack of funeral goods.

The entire necropolis is laid out around a small building for Christian worship situated behind the Hellenistic building of the stoa. It is a *cella memoriae,* a church built in remembrance of an important person connected with the primitive Christian community of Empúries, who was buried inside the church. It was built during the 4th century, taking advantage of the remains of the ancient Roman thermal installations which were still standing. Therefore, the wall that closed off the nave of the *cella* to the north had the typical vaulted niches of rooms in Roman baths, and its floor (made from pieces of marble) is none other than the old floor of the thermal installations. The *cella memoriae* is a building with just one nave, having a presbytery with an apse that was semicircular inside and rectangular outside. On the northern side of this apse there is small room for liturgical use, possibly a vestry. In the centre of the sanctuary, under the altar, was the sepulchre of the Christian person in question, unfortunately unknown to us, to whom the building of the *cella* was dedicated. His sepulchre was the famous sarcophagus of the Seasons, found during the excavations organised by the Diputació of Girona in 1846-1848, and which can currently be seen in the Museu d'Arqueologia de Catalunya-Girona. It was a

A marble foot of an altar from the Visigothic period, decorated in relief. It is uncertain where it came from, but it could have been in one of the buildings for worship in Sant Martí d'Empúries.

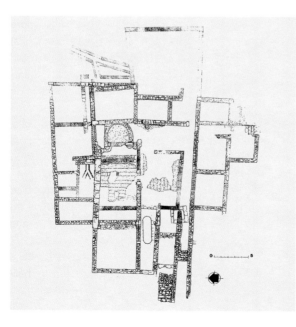

Plan of the structures corresponding to the Late Roman building for worship, with nearby funeral chambers (according to Nolla and Sagrera 1996).

sculpted marble sarcophagus, of a high artistic quality, produced in a Roman workshop at the beginning of the 4th century. It has a pagan theme, and was without doubt, re-used and moved to this place at the time this Christian building was built.

To the south of the nave, a very wide vestibule gave access to the liturgical areas. Around the *cella memoriae*, you can see a series of rooms that were re-used as funeral chambers, in which there are a series of sarcophaguses made of stone with double-sloped lids and six decorative acroteria in contrast to the poorness of the majority of Emporitan burials. Both the religious building and the funeral chambers were at a much lower level than the exterior, which is why they were reached by stairs at the end of the vestibule.

## Sant Martí d'Empúries: the nucleus of the Late Roman and Mediaeval city of Empúries

From the 3rd century the city of Empúries, as we have mentioned, was concentrated in the area where there is now the present village of Sant Martí d'Empúries, the ancient *Palaiapolis* from the classical period. Surrounded by its city walls, Empúries was, throughout the whole of the Late Antiquity, the seat of the important bishopric of the same name, a commercial and political centre covering a wide territory, and a port enclave. Contrary to the belief of traditional historiography, Empúries kept its port installations active, and commercialised through them, amongst other products, amphorae from Africa, the Orient and the south of peninsula, transporting oil, wine or salted fish, and crockery from Africa, the Orient and the south of Gaul, which were documented during the course of the excavations. Unfortunately, our knowledge of the city of Empúries during this period is very poor due to the superimposition of the present village on its remains. Archaeological excavations carried out to date in Sant Martí have only allowed us to document some structures for living and storing purposes for this period, and to identify a part of the face of the Late Roman wall, on a plot of land next to the present church. This data is obviously too sparse to be able to suggest the urban layout of the city and the location of its main buildings.

Sculpted marble sarcophagus with symbolic representations of the Seasons on either side of the image of the deceased. The front of the lid is decorated with scenes of grape harvesting and wine and oil pressing. This was made in a Roman workshop at the beginning of the 4ᵗʰ century. Although the motifs are of pagan origin, it was re-used for the main tomb in the small Paleo-Christian church in the Neapolis. It is currently on display at the Museu d'Arqueologia de Catalunya – Girona (Jordi S. Carrera).

The fact that Empúries was a bishop's seat, documented at least from the 516 council held in Tarragona, which *Paulus*, the first of the known Emporitan bishops, attended, implies the existence of a whole series of ecclesiastic structures (a church, a bishop's palace and baptistery) which have not been discovered. One hypothesis is that the Episcopal basilica could have been under the present church of Sant Martí d'Empúries, but there is no evidence to support this.

The Muslim invasion of Empúries, in about 715, marked the beginning of a new period in history. Towards 785, with the outright conquest of Girona, the territory of the Empordà came under Carolingian control. The reorganisation of the Hispanic territories in 812 led to the creation of the Mediaeval County of Empúries, with Ermenguer as its first known Count. In Empúries, as the county capital bearing the same name, the count resided with his court. Although the ancient bishopric seat was not re-established, the political and military importance of the city were great, being mainly based on maintaining the port structures. In about 1064 the capital of the county was moved to Castelló d'Empúries, which meant a decrease in the

View of the archaeological excavations in the Plaça Petita (the small square) in Sant Martí d'Empúries in 1994. You can see the remains of a Late Roman wall.

importance of Empúries as an urban nucleus. Thus Empúries, dependent on Castelló, was reduced to being simply a fortified place.

We do not know the layout of the city during this period. The walls that are visible these days are the result of continuous rebuilding up to the beginning of the modern era. The church was repeatedly rebuilt as can be seen by two inscriptions on its face that inform us of a reconstruction started in 926 by Count Gausbert and a series of reforms made by the sacristan Guillem de Palol in 1248. The present church is a very simple Late Gothic building, started in 1507 according to the inscription on its face. Inside the church there are two interesting altars from the Paleo-Christian period and a third one, with a decoration of alveolae, which show its continued use as a place of Christian worship.

Both in Late Antiquity and during the High Mediaeval period, the city of Empúries was surrounded by a number of small rural establishments that constituted an important and dispersed population. Evidence of this suburban population is documented both by the existence of the different necropolises that are not directly related to the city, and by the presence of the structural remains of occupation, in most cases not at all well known, that included small churches for worship.

Amongst the Late Roman cemeteries of Empúries we should mention the Estruch necropolis, to the south-west of the hill occupied by the Roman city, with a typology of diverse burials that go as far as the road to Sant Martí d'Empúries. The necropolis of Castellet, on the les Corts hill (to the south of the Roman city) also dates from that same period, and it is laid out around a funeral monument in the form of a tower, the remains of which are still visible today. Of the dwellings and religious buildings that have survived, the best known all belong to the High Middle Ages, but they are very probably built on structures from a previous period. Therefore, it is interesting to visit the two churches that are situated alongside the road to Sant Martí d'Empúries, having turned off the road from Orriols to L'Escala.

The church of Santa Magdalena, in the eastern sector of this area, is a small building with a rectangular apse (covered with a vault and at a higher level than the rest of the building), a transversal room and a single nave with a side entrance to the south, with a series of funeral chambers backing on to the church. The current construction is the result of various reforms that, chronologically, can be dated back to the 10th century. Despite this, we know today that the origin of this church is a funeral site from the Late Roman period, and that in the 6th century it was adapted as a building for Christian worship, and around which the burial necropolis shaped itself.

A hundred metres to the west of Santa Magdalena we find the remains of Santa Margarida. This is also a small building, in the shape of a rectangular hall and a horseshoe apse covered with a vault, which must date back to

**The churches and suburban cemeteries**

**32**

**31**

Aerial view of the church of
Santa Magdalena.

the end of the 10th century. The church was built on top of previous buildings, amongst which we should mention a square piscina, probably belonging to a baptistery from the 6th century, which at the same time had been built over an older burial cemetery which we know as the Estruch necropolis, and which we have mentioned before. These earlier remains made up part of a building complex that extended to the nearby cultivated fields and

Aerial view of the church of
Santa Margarida.

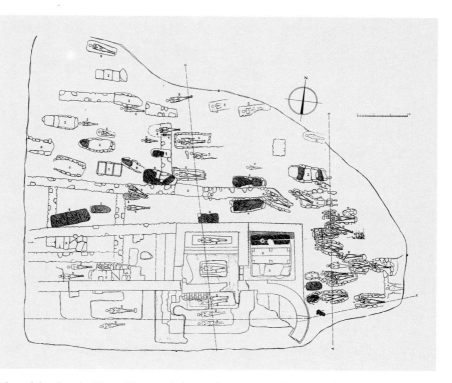

Plan of the church of Sant Vicenç and the nearby cemetery, situated at the base of the western part of les Corts hill.

that until further archaeological investigations offer more information, are even more difficult to interpret. It should be pointed out that a fragment of strigilated sarcophagus came from here; it was from an Aquitanian workshop and can be dated to the 5th or 6th century, representing a chrismon circled by a triple crown of laurel leaves, and is on display in the Museum of Empúries.

Finally, it is interesting to comment on the existence of the church of Sant Vicenç, at the foot of the eastern sector of les Corts hill. It is a church with just one nave, with a semicircular apse and transept, dating back to the second half of the 9th century or the 10th century. It had an important burial necropolis around it, and we cannot rule out the existence of previous structures and burials, as

**34**

Remains of the tower-like funeral monument at the top of les Corts hill. In Late Roman times there was a cemetery around it, that must be related to some of the nuclei that existed around Empúries.

would seem to be the case of a stone sarcophagus with a double-sloping top and decorative acroterium, such as those found next to the *cella memoriae* of the Emporitan Neapolis. The second piece of strigilated Aquitanian sarcophagus from one of the farmhouses near this church is on display in the Museum, in this case it is decorated with a crater.

This whole perspective, to which we must also add the rural settlement of Cinc Claus with its High Mediaeval church dedicated to Santa Reparada, helps us to understand the close relationship between the city of Empúries and its immediate surroundings during those periods of time about which we know so little.

## Modern Empúries and the beginning of the excavations

After human activity had become concentrated in the nucleus of Sant Martí, the ancient *Palaiapolis,* and after the transfer of the county capital to Castelló d'Empúries, silence and forgetfulness erased the memory of the past of the city, and even of its very

2 Excavacions d'Empuries — Museu de la Excma · Diputació Provincial de Barcelona

Photograph by J. Esquirol, taken in 1916, showing the remains of the church built by the Servite monks, later re-used for the present Museum building.

existence. It was not until the end of the 15th century that the Bishop of Girona, Joan Margarit, would identify the exact location of the old city of Empúries, but unfortunately this was soon forgotten.

A hundred years later, throughout the 16th century, a small group of fishermen from Empúries (which is now Sant Martí) started to settle in the place that was to become L'Escala, making the most of its excellent port conditions. At the same time as L'Escala d'Empúries was being consolidated as a nucleus, the ancient Emporitan site was once again inhabited. In 1606, a community of Servite monks built a monastery and a church dedicated to Our Lady of Gracia, on the land that covered the remains of the Neapolis. As a result of the "decree of Mendizabal", they left the convent in 1835. Although we do not have any evidence about the monastery, the remains of the church which has been restored are currently home to the Museum of Empúries and other services.

View of the site at
Empúries, as it is today.

Three years after the installation of the Servite monks in the ruins of Empúries, Jeroni Pujades correctly identified the location of the ancient Greek and Roman city, and from this time its location would not be forgotten and would become part of the historic references collected in various publications in the 17th, 18th and 19th centuries. On the other hand, since the last quarter of the 17th century the town of L'Escala became firmly established, and substituted the old city of Empúries as the main nucleus of the population. Josep Maranges de Marimón, a local from L'Escala, wrote the first monograph on Empúries, *"Compendio histórico, resumen y descripción de la anti-quísima ciudad de Empurias" ("A historical compendium, a summary and description of the ancient city of Empúries")*, published in 1803.

It was not until the 19th century was well under way that the first official archaeological excavations were started. Apart from private research, such as that done by the Servite monk, Manuel Romeu at the beginning of that century, the County Commission of Monuments of Girona, under the control of the Diputació de Girona, started a series of excavations between 1846 and 1848 around the *cella memoriae* from the Paleo-Christian period of the Neapolis. The Diputació de Girona did not consider it was of sufficient interest to continue with the archaeological research and from that moment their only action was to buy some objects from the numerous clandestine excavations that proliferated throughout the whole of the second half of the 19th century and the beginning of the last one, and which amounted to a systematic plundering of a great part of the Emporitan necropolises.

Effective public intervention to safeguard and recover the archaeological site of Empúries started in 1907 when, thanks to the initiative of the architect Josep Puig i Cadafalch, the President of the Diputació de Barcelona, Enric Prat de la Riba, decided to start the necessary proceedings to buy the land around Empúries, and to subsidise the campaigns of systematic excavation, through the Junta de Museus of Barcelona, which had just been created by the Diputació and the Town Council of Barcelona. This interest in recovering the classical past of Catalonia is part of the intellectual movement known as "Noucentisme", and was possible thanks to the foresight of Prat de la Riba. On March 23rd 1908, once the first lands had been acquired, excavations on the fields started under the scientific direction of Puig i Cadafalch, and the direct responsibility of his representative Emili Gandia. During the first campaign, the archaeological work was carried out around the area of the southern wall of the Roman city and the southern sector of the Greek city. The following year, however, work was based mainly in the Neapolis. On October 25th 1909, the discovery of the statue of Asclepius meant a new impulse for research and the archaeological safekeeping of Empúries, an aspect of the recovery of our collective past that has continued almost without interruption to the present.

# Bibliography

**AAVV**, *Imatges d'Empúries*, Barcelona, 1993.

**AAVV**, *Intervencions arqueològiques a Sant Martí d'Empúries (1994-1996). De l'assentament precolonial a l'Empúries actual,* Monografies Emporitanes, 9, Girona, 1999.

**M. ALMAGRO**, *Las fuentes escritas referentes a Ampurias*, Monografías Ampuritanas, I, Barcelona, 1951.

**M. ALMAGRO**, *Las inscripciones ampuritanas griegas, ibéricas y latinas*, Monografías Ampuritanas, II, Barcelona, 1952.

**M. ALMAGRO**, *Las necrópolis de Ampurias (2 vols.)*, Monografías Ampuritanas, III, Barcelona, 1953-1955.

**M. ALMAGRO**, *Excavaciones en la Palaiápolis de Ampurias*, Excavaciones Arqueológicas en España, 27, Madrid, 1964.

**X. AQUILUÉ, R. MAR, J. M. NOLLA, J. RUIZ DE ARBULO, E. SANMARTÍ,** *El fòrum romà d'Empúries (Excavacions de l'any 1982). Una aproximació arqueològica al procés històric de la romanització al nord-est de la península ibèrica,* Monografies Emporitanes, VI, Barcelona, 1984.

**J. ARXÉ**, *Les llànties tardo-republicanes d'Empúries*, Monografies Emporitanes, V, Barcelona, 1982.

**L. BURÉS**, *Les estructures hidràuliques a la ciutat antiga: L'exemple d'Empúries*, Monografies Emporitanes, 10, Barcelona, 1998.

**R. MAR, J. RUIZ DE ARBULO**, *Ampurias romana. Historia, Arquitectura y Arqueología*, Sabadell, 1993.

**R. MARCET, E. SANMARTÍ**, *Empúries*, Barcelona, 1989.

**J. M. NOLLA, J. CASAS**, *Carta arqueològica de les comarques de Girona. El poblament d'època romana al nord-est de Catalunya*, Girona, 1983.

**J. M. NOLLA, J. SAGRERA**, *Ciuitatis Impuritanae Coementeria. Les necròpolis tardanes de la Neàpolis*, Estudi General, 15 (1995), Revista de la Facultat de Lletres, Universitat de Girona, Girona, 1996.

**E. SANMARTÍ**, *La cerámica campaniense de Emporion y Rhode*, Monografies Emporitanes, IV, Barcelona, 1978.

**E. SANMARTÍ**, Bibliografia ampuritana 1901-1995, *Cypsela*, XI, Girona, 1996, pp. 161-173.

**Acroterium:** Decorative element, of stone or terracotta, placed on the highest point of the pediment in Greek, Etruscan and Roman temples, in the shape of a palmette or a figure.

**Agora:** Public square in ancient Greek cities which was the centre of political, commercial and civic life.

**Alae:** Literally wings in Latin. When referring to a Roman house this term describes two open areas, one on either side of the atrium, in which, according to tradition, family records and images of predecessors were originally kept.

**Antefix:** In classical architecture a decorative element made of stone or more often of terracotta, in the shape of a palmette or a figure, which was placed above the cornices to hide the edge of the roof tiles.

**Atrium:** Nucleus of the traditional Italic house, usually with a semi-covered interior court around which the rooms were built. The opening in the roof or compluvium allowed light, air and rainwater to come in. The rainwater was collected in a small impluvium or tank in the centre of the floor, from where it could be sent to underground cisterns.

**Cardo:** A Latin word Roman surveyors used to define the north to south axes, also used for the names of the streets that went from north to south in Roman cities. The expression *Cardo Maximus* refers to the main street or axis of the city.

**Cella:** An interior area in a classical temple where the images of the deity were kept.

**Cella memoriae:** Small temple or edicule usually linked to the memory of some person who was significant in the early Christian communities, especially concerning worshipping a martyr. They used to be built in cemeteries of the Paleo-Christian period.

**Chrismon:** The monogram representing the name of Christ formed by joining the first two letters, XP, of his Greek name (Χριστος). Sometimes the Greek letters alpha (Α) and omega (Ω) are shown either side, referring to the beginning and the end of all things. This motif is very frequent in Paleo-Christian symbolism, and can be found on sarcophaguses, paintings, illustrations on pottery, and so on.

**Crater:** A medium-sized Greek vase, which was used for mixing water and wine in the symposium ritual or banquet ceremony. It was like a large goblet with a base and two handles, although there were variations on this shape.

**Cremation:** Funeral rite consisting of cremating or burning the body.

**Cryptoportico:** An underground passageway or gallery that was usually a substructure for a portico above. It was frequently used in the architecture of the public forum in Roman cities, although it was also used in some domestic buildings.

**Domus:** A Latin word meaning a house or family dwelling, generally within the urban area.

**Drachma:** Coin issued by the ancient Greek cities, the name of which has been preserved to the present day as the currency in modern Greece. It was a silver coin, worth six oboli, which had different kinds of inscriptions which often made reference to the issuing city, its origin, the main religious worship, and so on.

**Edicule:** A small building, usually of a religious nature, like a small temple.

**Forum:** Civic centre of Roman cities, which was used as a centre for the main religious, political and administrative events of the community. Its nucleus was made up of the public square (*area),* around which the most representative public buildings of the city were built.

**Inhumation:** Funeral rite consisting of burying the body.

**Insulae:** A Latin word used to designate the islands created by the layout of the roads in ancient cities. They were square or rectangular and varied in size according to the urban layout and characteristics.

**Opus caementicium:** Latin expression referring to a very solid type of construction, consisting of walls with a nucleus made of mortar or plaster mixed with stones (*caementa).*

**Opus signinum:** Latin expression referring to a type of very common flooring characterised by a plaster finish mixed with small pieces of crushed pottery. It was often decorated with tesserae arranged in simple geometric designs. Due to its hardwearing properties and the fact that it was waterproof it was also used to line cisterns, pipes and other water-related constructions.

**Peristyle:** A court surrounded by columned porticoes that was a characteristic element of Greek-Hellenistic houses. From the 2nd century BC this same architectural feature was introduce into Italic atrium houses. However, the columns were usually placed around a small interior garden, and grouped around the porticoes were the most important rooms of the house.

**Pronaos:** Greek word meaning space, usually preceded by a columned portico, which was used as a anteroom to the nave or interior area of a temple.

**Stoa:** A building with a portico, with one or more rows of columns, built around the agorae in Greek and Hellenistic cities, for social and commercial activities.

**Strigil:** A metal tool, with a curved blade and a handle, used by the Greeks and the Romans to remove sweat, oil, ointments and so on from their bodies, after gymnastic exercises or during the thermal baths. By analogy, the name was also given to a type of decorative motif in the shape of a sinuous S-shaped stria or groove that was frequently used as decoration on Paleo-Christian sarcophaguses.

**Tabernae**: Latin word for business premises for varied handicraft and commercial activities, which lined the streets in Roman cities.

**Tablinum:** Main reception area in traditional Italic houses, at the back of the atrium, in front of the entrance, where the head of the family (*dominus*) received visitors and customers.

**Triclinium:** Name given to the room used for meals and banquets, where the guests lay on U-shaped beds (*lectus triclinaris*) around the table or tables where the food was served. Originally from Greece, this kind of room became a characteristic element of noble Roman houses, where supper (*cena*) was a very important part of the social activities of its owners.

# General Information

## Information and reservations

Museu d'Arqueologia de Catalunya-Empúries

Apartat de correus 21,

17130 l'Escala,

Tel. 972 77 02 08

Fax. 972 77 42 60

http://www.mac.es

e-mail: empuries@mac.es

## Site opening hours

October 1st to May 31st.

Seven days a week from 10am to 6 pm.

June 1st to September 30th

Seven days a week from 10am to 8 pm.

During the week leading up to Easter the site will open as in the summer.

Closed on January 1st and December 25th

## Information Office and Educational Services

Museu d'Arqueologia de Catalunya-Barcelona

Passeig de Santa Madrona, 39

08038 Barcelona

Tel. +34 93 424 65 77 / 93 423 212 49

Fax. +34 93 424 56 30

## Nearby places of interest

Sant Marti d'Empúries (1km). Small Mediaeval village. Ancient island on which the Greeks established their first settlement (*Palaiapolis*).

The Greek jetty (500m). On the beach of Sant Martí.

The churches of Santa Margarida and Santa Magdalena (1km). On the west slope of Empúries hill, along the road leading to Sant Martí. Different settlements from the Late Roman and High Mediaeval periods.

Les Corts hill (1km). Funeral monument from the Roman period.

L'Escala (1km). Important modern-day port and tourist centre. The town was founded in the 16th century by the old fishermen of Empúries.

Pals (30km). Mediaeval village.

Ullastret (25km). Ruins of an Iberian settlement.

Peretallada (30km). Mediaeval village.

Aiguamolls de l'Empordà Natural Park (15km).

Castelló d'Empúries (23km). Old capital of the Mediaeval county of Empúries from the 11th century. Magnificent Gothic cathedral.

Peralada (35km). Mediaeval nucleus.

Figueres (25km). Dalí Museum.

Sant Pere de Rodes (55km). 11th century monastery.

Roses (40km). Old fishing village, seat of the ancient Greek colony of Rhode.

Vilabertran Monastery (28km).

## How to reach Empúries

By bus to L'Escala, 1km from Empúries:
Figueres-Sant Pere Pescador-L'Escala line.
Girona-L'Escala line.
Girona-L'Estartit line.
Barcelona-Costa Brava line.

SARFA offices (bus company)
Girona 972 201796
Figueres 972 674298
L'Escala 972 770218
Barcelona 93 265 1158

By train:
The main line goes from Barcelona-Girona-Figueres.
Information RENFE (national train company):
Barcelona 93 490 0202
Girona 972 207093
Figueres 972 504661
Portbou 972 3000099

By car:
A-7 Motorway, Barcelona-La Jonquera
(L'Escala-Empúries exit)
N-11, Barcelona-La Jonquera
C-252, Corça-Portbou
C-260, Besalú-Roses

© **Text**
Xavier Aquilué Abadías, Pere Castanyer Masoliver, Marta Santos
Retolaza and Joaquim Tremoleda Trilla

© **Fotographs and illustrations**
The authors or the institutions and people mentioned in the text.

Photographic Archive of M.A.C.-Empúries
Jordi S. Carrera
J. Esquirol
J. M. Nolla
J. Sagrera

© **Published by**
Museu d'Arqueologia de Catalunya

Edicions El Mèdol
Cartagena 15-A. 43004 Tarragona

**Graphic design**
Josep M. Mir
Collaborators: Marta Bachs and Jaume Sellarés

**Application of the graphic design**
Josep Salvadó Monseny

**Translation**
Veronica Lambert Hall

**Revision of archaeological terms:**
Marta Santos

Depósito legal: T-1221-2000
ISBN: 84.95559-03

**First edition:** August 2000